What Your Cat
is Thinking

What Your Cat is Thinking

Everything you need to know
to understand your pet

BO SÖDERSTRÖM

First published in Sweden in 2017 by Bonnier Fakta as *Hur tänker din katt?*
This edition published in 2019 by John Murray Learning,
an imprint of Hodder & Stoughton. An Hachette UK Company.

Copyright © Bo Söderström 2019
Translation by Daniel Lind

The right of Bo Söderström to be identified as the Author of the Work has
been asserted by him in accordance with the Copyright, Designs and
Patents Act 1988.

Author photo © Stefan Tell
Photo credits: page xii © Bo Söderström; throughout the book © Shutterstock.com
Illustrations © Anders Rådén; cat silhouettes designed by Renata.s / Freepik

A CIP catalogue record for this title is available from the British Library.

Paperback ISBN: 978 1 473 68980 0
eBook ISBN: 978 1 473 68982 4

1

Typeset by Cenveo® Publisher Services.

Printed and bound in Great Britain by Clays Ltd, Elcograf S.p.A.

John Murray Learning policy is to use papers that are natural, renewable and recyclable
products and made from wood grown in sustainable forests. The logging and manu-
facturing processes are expected to conform to the environmental regulations of the
country of origin.

Carmelite House
50 Victoria Embankment
London EC4Y 0DZ
www.johnmurraypress.co.uk

Contents

Preface

I HAD THE idea for this book one Saturday at the beginning of 2015, as I listened to 'Lundström's Book Radio' on Swedish Radio's channel P1. The programme looked into the future: what books will take over when the Nordic noir craze wears off? Several people mentioned a growing interest in books about our pets and how they behave. On the same day the newspaper *Dagens Nyheter* reported on a study about why cats are so fond of empty boxes. It was the most shared article on social media that weekend. A thought struck me: why not write a book that summarizes all the research into cat behaviour? My starting point couldn't have been better: I've had the privilege of living with a cat almost all my life; I have a background as a scientist in ecology; and I'm used to extracting the essential information from the impenetrable language that researchers use. It's important to me that study results also benefit everyone. It has been great fun to write about the multifaceted cat, and I hope that joy permeates this book.

More than half of all households in the Western world have a pet. In both Europe and the USA, the cat has surpassed the dog as the most common pet. In 2012 there were 90 million cats in Europe and 74 million in the USA. Our fascination and admiration for cats know no bounds; we only have to look at the massive numbers of pictures and videos of cats on the Internet!

Bo Söderström

Introduction

CATS ARE WHAT they are and they behave as they like, wrote the Swedish poet and writer Aase Berg in her account of the cat's role in literature. We humans try to understand the cat and how it perceives reality. What does the cat really think? Is it domesticated or wild? We share our fascination with felines with authors such as Werner Aspenström, T. S. Eliot and Doris Lessing. Lessing, especially, was an eagle-eyed observer of cat behaviour; her observations of how Rufus, an old fighter, took his place among the other cats in her home are a joy to read.

Just like many other cat lovers, I have a fair number of books about cat behaviour on my shelves. Why yet another book about cats, then? Most books about cats, regardless of who wrote them, are based upon the author's own experiences of how his or her darling behaves. The interpretations might be correct in many cases, but cats are individuals after all, with varied behaviours. That's why it's more reliable to present the results from controlled studies of many different cats' individual behaviours.

Cats don't behave wilfully. They show clear behavioural patterns, which are revealed through careful research studies. That is why this book is needed.

We are sitting on a treasure trove of research about cats' behaviour. A simple search of the world's largest database of scientific literature (Web of Science) reveals many articles about why cats do what they do. Unfortunately, these results are rarely released to the wider public from the researchers' ivory towers. Researchers usually write for the benefit of other researchers in a complicated and impenetrable language. The public, though, has a hunger for this knowledge, as is shown by the impact of news articles that describe the results of cat research.

This book describes the most exciting research studies and their conclusions in an accessible way. You'll get practical tips on what to do in order for you and your cat to get along better. I explain, for example, how you should stroke your cat to make it feel really good, and how to prevent your darling from scratching the furniture. My hope is that you will also become even more fascinated by your cat as you learn about its history and how it adapted to life with people. Was it the human that domesticated the cat or did the cat domesticate itself? How big a threat to wild birds, voles and mice is the predatory cat? What influence do cats have on our physical and mental wellbeing? By asking these and other questions about the cat, we can even learn something about ourselves along the way. I learned a lot while working on the book, despite having lived with one or more cats for most of my life. And the research I mention is hot off the press; some research areas have expanded hugely lately and a large number of articles have been written since 2010. Enjoy!

The science behind this book

When I undertook a search of scientific articles about cat behaviour in Web of Science, in February 2015, the search terms *domestic cat* and *behaviour* gave me 800 articles. I downloaded and read the summaries of all these articles from the database. They gave a good indication of the content, and I used this information to select the most interesting articles to read in full. My focus was on articles that piqued my curiosity. I read more than a hundred articles, through which I found even more articles that seemed exciting. I stopped at about 140 articles, which could be naturally divided into six themes that comprise the chapters of this book: 'The wild in the tame', 'Your cat's senses', 'Your cat's behaviour', 'Your cat's temperament', 'The cat and the human' and 'The cat at home'. I made three to six further divisions to create sub-sections within each theme.

The book has 30 of these subsections in total, which are based on results and conclusions from a variety of research articles: about 20 each for the sections entitled 'The predatory cat' and 'Your cat's health and wellbeing', but just one each for the sections entitled 'Tail in the air' and 'Hairballs'. Surprisingly enough, I didn't find any exciting articles about the cat's sight. Articles about sight focused on various eye diseases or the physiology of the cat eye. I wanted to spare you that. I don't claim this book will cover all the cat's various behaviours, but it was the availability of interesting articles that was conclusive. All the articles that form the basis for the book are listed chapter by chapter in the reference section at the back of the book.

The number of articles about our domesticated animals' behaviours came as a big surprise. The scientific foundation for most other pets is even larger than that for cats. For example, more than 1,000 articles have been written about dog behaviour and 5,000 about horses. Much of this research from around the world has been funded by taxes. In other words, it's you and I who have paid for it. It's only fair that we get to see the results.

The number of articles published in scientific journals has increased dramatically in recent years. Not even researchers themselves have time to scan through a fraction of everything that is being published. There are both gems and duds. And it's important to examine the articles critically to form your own opinion. Despite the system's shortcomings, the scientific method is unparalleled: the theoretical basis and how the research will contribute to increased knowledge are declared; and the researchers describe what they've done to answer their hypotheses.

The media are sometimes a little too dramatic when they report on current research. Recently I saw the headline 'Your Cat's Evil Plan – it probably wants to kill you' in Sweden's most read newspaper. In this book you will get the background and can form your own opinions on the truth behind the headlines.

Most studies I mention in this book have been controlled experiments. In other words, they have randomly divided cats into a trial group and a control group. The researchers make all circumstances between the two groups as equal as possible, except for the factor they want to test. After that, they systematically describe behaviours or measure something within the two groups. The researchers then compare the outcome of each group with the help of statistics. This is why a large sample of cats is needed in each group, so that the cats with outlying behaviours don't give a distorted picture of the group as a whole.

Different kinds of cats

The scientific articles that are the basis for this book described studies of different kinds of domesticated cats, and the researchers have not been particularly good at defining clearly what sort of cats they've been studying. To make it easier for you as the reader, I will use only three groups of cats in this book: the house cat, the farm cat and the feral cat.

The house cat lives in a household where the owners take responsibility for giving it food and shelter. It can live alone or in a group and sleeps in the home. The indoor cat is a domesticated cat that isn't allowed outside at all, while the outdoor cat goes out whenever it feels like it. A mixed-breed cat is a domesticated cat without a pedigree, while a pure-bred cat is a domesticated cat that has one.

The farm cat is loosely tied to a farm and always lives in a group. It seldom or never sleeps in the home and receives food irregularly from the human. There's obviously a sliding scale between farm cat and domesticated cat.

The feral cat may look like a domesticated or farm cat, but it is obviously not its appearance that is decisive here but its behaviour. Vets describe a feral cat as an animal you can't approach in nature, and one that can survive without any human involvement. It may have been either born in the wild, without knowing humans, or previously domesticated but later abandoned. A captured feral cat may be aggressive, or it may cower and try to hide. You cannot handle a feral cat even when it's captured.

Domesticated and farm cats mate more often with feral cats than one might think. The European wildcat also mates with domesticated cats in those areas where their domains overlap, and their offspring are fertile. The European wildcat can be found in Scotland, eastern France, Spain, Italy and large areas of the Balkans.

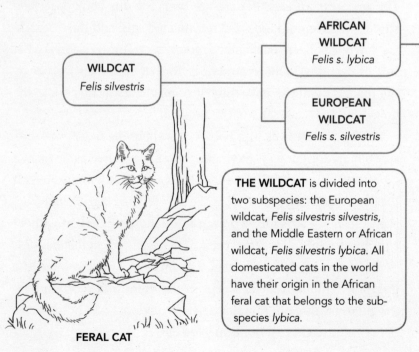

WILDCAT
Felis silvestris

AFRICAN WILDCAT
Felis s. lybica

EUROPEAN WILDCAT
Felis s. silvestris

THE WILDCAT is divided into two subspecies: the European wildcat, *Felis silvestris silvestris*, and the Middle Eastern or African wildcat, *Felis silvestris lybica*. All domesticated cats in the world have their origin in the African feral cat that belongs to the subspecies *lybica*.

FERAL CAT

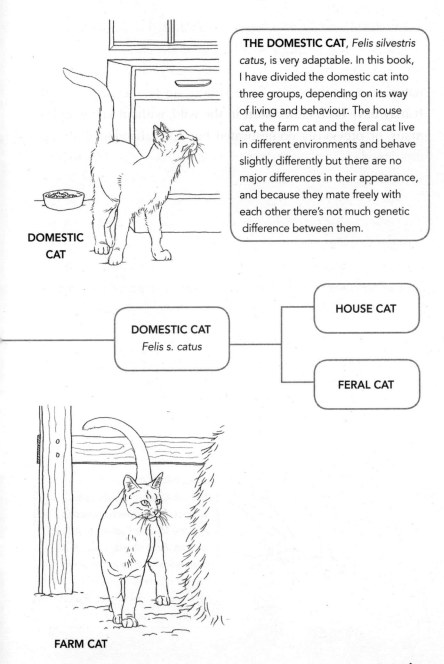

THE DOMESTIC CAT, *Felis silvestris catus*, is very adaptable. In this book, I have divided the domestic cat into three groups, depending on its way of living and behaviour. The house cat, the farm cat and the feral cat live in different environments and behave slightly differently but there are no major differences in their appearance, and because they mate freely with each other there's not much genetic difference between them.

DOMESTIC CAT

HOUSE CAT

DOMESTIC CAT
Felis s. catus

FERAL CAT

FARM CAT

1

The wild in the tame

NEW RESEARCH INDICATES that humans haven't yet domesticated the cat. At least, we haven't managed to breed desirable behaviours and appearances in the cat to the degree we have done with dogs and other pets. We've accepted the cat's peculiarities and the cat has, in turn, accepted our ways. This chapter describes the primal behaviours that still exist within the domesticated cat.

More wild than tame?

Your cat sleeps calmly on a pillow in the kitchen and doesn't care at all that the dog is barking and people are bustling about with dinner preparations. In the past, this scene would be unthinkable for a wild predator like the cat. Humans and dogs were real threats to a feline, and it would keep its distance from human settlements as well as it could. How, then, did this wild animal adjust to a life with humans? Thanks to breeding, other species that started as wild have had their attributes and behaviours changed to be desirable ones for us. Cows, pigs, goats, sheep, chickens, horses and dogs are all examples of animals the human has domesticated. But how much has the cat been domesticated? Is the cat lying in your kitchen really more domesticated than wild?

Charles Darwin noted, towards the end of the nineteenth century, that domesticated animals have common traits. Their brains are smaller and they have more juvenile traits – that is, they behave more like youngsters than adults – in comparison to their wild ancestors. There are examples of dog breeds where the adult dog reminds you of a puppy, with its short nose, big eyes and floppy ears. Interestingly enough, researchers believe this to be a by-product of the fact that humans have tried to breed animals with good behaviours. We've got animals with a youthful appearance and a smaller brain as part of the bargain, so to speak. This, at least, is the theory recently put forward by researchers in comparative genomics. In this field, researchers first map the genetic material in an organism and then compare the genes and their expression between species.

The first study of a cat's genetic material was published in the American journal *Proceedings of the National Academy of Sciences* in 2014. An American research team led by Michael Montague found 281 genes in an Abyssinian female cat that showed signs of rapid change. Some of these genes were connected to the cat's sight and hearing, the senses on which a cat most depends. Other genes were involved in the circulation of fats in the body, which is probably an adaptation from when cats ate only meat. But the most interesting results appeared when the researchers compared the genetic material of 22 different domesticated cats (from different breeds and geographical locations) with the genetic material in the cat's ancestors (two wildcats from Europe of subspecies *Felis silvestris silvestris* and two from the Middle East of the subspecies *Felis silvestris lybica*). At least 13 genes differed between wild and domesticated cats. From earlier studies on mice we know that these genes delineate behaviours, such as being less frightened in unfamiliar situations and the ability to learn new things when rewarded with food.

Compared to the dog, the cat has gone through a less intensive change in its genetic material and it happened more recently (see the table below). The researchers concluded their article by stating that humans haven't actively domesticated the cat in the same way as they have dogs and other pets. The cat merely followed the human, and the human tolerated it.

But then, you might say, humans have bred many different cat breeds. This is correct, but of the approximately 40 to 50 different cat breeds existing today, most of them are less than 75 years old. At the very first cat show – in the Crystal Palace, London, in 1871 – only five different breeds were presented: the Birman, the British Shorthair, the Manx, the Persian and the Siamese. Between most of today's breeds there are only a few minor differences in the genetic material, usually just a single gene separating them.

When did the different cat breeds appear?

600–1200	1300–1800	1800–1900	1950–TODAY
Japanese Bobtail	Burmese	Abyssinian	American Bobtail
	Korat	Birman	American Shorthair
	Siamese	British Shorthair	American Wirehair
	Turkish Angora	Maine Coon	Australian Mist
		Manx	Cornish Rex
		Norwegian Forest	Devon Rex
		Persian	Egyptian Mau
		Russian Blue	LaPerm
		Siberian	Munchkin
		Turkish Van	Ocicat
			Ojos Azules
			Ragdoll
			Scottish Fold
			Selkirk Rex
			Sphynx
			Tonkinese

Selective breeding to vary the cat's appearance has taken place over a very short period compared to the length of time – at least 9,500 years – that humans and cats have associated with each other. Even if appearances may differ between cat breeds, they all have quite primal behaviours: 'You can take the cat out of the jungle, but not the jungle out of the cat!' if you will.

Where in the world did the wildcat first learn to live as the human's companion? To answer this question, an English research group led by Carlos Driscoll compared how various subspecies of the wildcat and the domestic cat were related. The results were published once more in the distinguished journal *Proceedings of the National Academy of Sciences.* Five different subspecies of *Felis silvestris* were used in the study: *silvestris* from Europe, *cafra* from Southern Africa, *ornata* from Central Asia, *lybica* from the Middle East and Africa, and *bieti* from the Tibetan Highlands. It turned out that all domestic cats in the world have their origin in the subspecies *lybica* from the Middle East. Images of cats 3,600 years old have been found in Egyptian graves. Archaeological findings of cat bones in settlements in Cyprus and Jericho in Palestine are even older than that – 9,500 and 8,700 years old, respectively.

Almost all of today's domesticated animals – cows, pigs, sheep and goats as well as dogs and cats – were domesticated in the same region about 8,000 to 12,000 years ago (see the map below). This region is in the Middle East and covers parts of areas that are now Israel, Palestine, Jordan, Lebanon, Syria, Turkey, Iran and Iraq. The most important waterways in this so-called Fertile Crescent are the Euphrates, Tigris and Jordan rivers. Today the area now is far from fertile, but in those days the landscape was a park-like savannah with scattered oak and pistachio trees. Humans settled here, and instead of hunting and gathering they became farmers. Wheat, corn, lentils, peas, chickpeas and other edible plants were cultivated. But why on earth would they domesticate an animal like the wildcat?

As Carlos Driscoll writes in the article: 'Wildcats are improbable candidates for domestication.' They eat nothing but meat, they live alone and defend territory, so they are more attached to places than people, they can't be trained to perform tasks, and they are not as good at hunting mice as some might believe, at least not compared to terriers and ferrets. As a matter of fact, farmers didn't even attempt to domesticate the cat, but tolerated it because at least it brought some benefit. Human and cat gradually accepted each other more and more. Why the cat sought out humans is easier to explain: it took advantage of a new ecological niche with plenty of food when mice, rats and sparrows were attracted to the humans' grain stores. There was little competition for the food because there weren't many other predators, and no larger predators that regarded the cat as prey.

Almost all house and farm cats in the world today are allowed to mate freely (unless neutered). The same applies to the numerous feral cats that mate regularly with our domesticated felines. Only a small proportion – around 3 per cent – of the world's domestic cats are pure bred, where we have actively chosen a mate for a cat to create desirable attributes in its offspring. Can we then truly say that we've domesticated the cat? Yes, the tolerance that domestic cats show towards people is a product of domestication. That domesticated cats can live in a group while the wildcat can only live alone is also a sign of

All domestic cats in the world have their origin in the wildcat from the subspecies lybica *in the Middle East. The oldest finds of cat bones in settlements are from Cyprus and Palestine, 9,500 and 8,700 years ago (dark dots). Mice, rats and sparrows congregated by grain stores, which the wildcat took advantage of. Almost all farmed animals were domesticated in the vicinity of the Fertile Crescent (pale grey) sometime between 8,000 and 12,000 years ago: the cow (dotted area), the pig (striped area), the sheep (mid-grey area) and the goat (dark grey).*

the cat's adaptability to a life with humans. And the profusion of new cat breeds we've seen during the past 75 years is definitely a result of us actively selecting desirable appearances and behaviours.

SCIENTISTS EXPLAIN

More wild than tame?

- The domestic cat has its origin in the African wildcat, *Felis silvestris*, of the subspecies *lybica* from the Middle East.
- The oldest archaeological finds of cat bones in settlements are 9,500 years old (from Cyprus).
- Humans also domesticated cows, pigs, sheep, goats and dogs for the first time in the Fertile Crescent in the Middle East.
- There are only 13 genes that differ between the domestic cat and the wildcat. These genes control behaviours like being less frightened in new situations and the ability to learn new things.
- The first farmers didn't try actively to domesticate the cat, but rather just tolerated the cat's presence. The cat domesticated itself!
- Active breeding to create new cat breeds is a modern phenomenon. Most of the 40–50 cat breeds known today are less than 75 years old.
- The domestic cat can mate with the wildcat and have fertile offspring.

How many cats should I have?

Probably the most common question I've had during my time writing this book is: 'I'm often out during the day and I feel bad that my cat is home alone. Should I get him another cat for company?'

Whereas the wildcat is solitary and keeps other wildcats away from its territory, the domestic cat can live alongside other cats. But is the house cat domesticated enough to enjoy living in a group, or does it merely tolerate the presence of other cats in the household?

In the Western world, it's become common for people to have more than one cat. For example, in 2012 there were an average of 2.1 cats per household in the USA and 1.6 cats per household in the UK. How do these cats feel? Many scientists have tackled this question, some by investigating stress hormones in the faeces and others by visiting people at home and studying their cats' behaviour – in both one-cat and multi-cat households.

Like other animals, a stressed cat produces the hormone cortisol, or glucocorticoid metabolites (GCMs), and various researchers have recently investigated how stressed a cat is by measuring the amount of GCMs in the urine or faeces. One of the most interesting studies is from Brazil, published in the journal *Physiology & Behavior* in 2013. Daniela Ramos and her colleagues investigated the level of stress hormone in the faeces of cats that lived in households with one, two, three and four cats.

The results showed large differences in stress between the cats, and within the same household. Different cats obviously react differently to the same kind of environment. But there were also clear patterns: stress levels were highest in cats between six months and two years old if they lived alone and lowest in households with two or three other cats. There were no discernible differences in the groups of cats older than two years old. How do we interpret these results? Researchers suggest that younger cats are able to satisfy their craving for play more easily in multi-cat households, whereas lone cats need their owner to provide stimuli with games and challenges. Older cats may have learned to tolerate – or avoid – each other, which means that they don't stress themselves if they have to share the household with other cats.

Humans play an important role in turning kittens into social creatures. We should handle kittens with care and be with them as much as possible from the age of two weeks until they're nine weeks old. They should also have the opportunity to socialize with other kittens and maybe even other adult cats in the household. During this short period, the kittens establish social behaviours that endure for the rest of their lives.

Several articles show that socialized kittens handle stressful situations more easily, such as being introduced into a household with unfamiliar people and even new cats and dogs. A new kitten will in most cases be more easily accepted than a new adult cat by older cats in a household, even if there's a risk that the elders don't always appreciate the wild playfulness of the kitten. However, researchers can't agree on whether to recommend a household with only male, only female or both genders of cat.

How, then, do cats who live with others behave in a household? To answer this question, the two behavioural ecologists Penny Bernstein and Mickie Strack locked themselves into a single-storey seven-room house with 14 cats. This study resembles the TV show *Big Brother*, with none of the cats allowed to leave the house while the experiment was in progress. The seven male and seven female cats were between six months and 13 years old and unknown to one another before the study; they weren't closely related; and all were neutered. Litter trays and dry food were present in all the rooms of the house, while wet food was given in the kitchen once a day.

Bernstein and Strack observed no clear hierarchy between the cats and open aggression was rare. The male cats created larger home areas and moved between more of the rooms than the females. Kittens moved freely in all the rooms at first, but by the end of the study they had limited their home area to one or two rooms. All the cats had found their favourite rooms after three months, except for one older male cat that still wandered like an unfriendly ghost from room to room.

Within each room the cats had their favourite spots to which they regularly returned. Often it was an elevated spot that was extra warm – maybe a shelf above a radiator or a mantelpiece. Several cats shared many of these favourite spots, which could have been a source of trouble, but the cats solved the problem in the same way that humans do with holiday apartments – instead of staying during different weeks, the cats used the same spot at different times of day. The researchers concluded that many cats are able to socialize in a limited space through a combination of tolerance and avoidance. Two conditions necessary for this to work were that the cats perceived that enough food was available and that there were safe havens to which they could withdraw when necessary.

Types of group behaviour in cats

SHARING A RESTING PLACE	CONTACT BEHAVIOUR	CONFLICT BEHAVIOUR	DIAGNOSIS	TREATMENT
Often	Licking each other Rubbing against each other	None		No treatment necessary
Seldom or never	Little or none	Avoiding each other and/or avoiding each other and/or chasing each other away from resting spots, but without any signs of anxiety or stress Might hiss and spit, but seldom leading to physical fights	Treatment necessary Cats don't need to be separated	An opportunity for cats to get away to an elevated spot in the room or a box on the floor Plenty of physical play and challenges Stopping mild conflicts with sudden loud noises Putting a collar with a bell on the attacker

SHARING A RESTING PLACE	CONTACT BEHAVIOUR	CONFLICT BEHAVIOUR	DIAGNOSIS	TREATMENT
Never	None	Can't see the other cat without becoming frightened, anxious or aggressive. Frequent physical fights that can lead to injury.	Treatment necessary Cats need to be separated	After the cats have been separated into different rooms, plan for a gradual reintroduction: rub a piece of cloth on the chin and temple of one of the cats and let the other cat smell it. Then do the same thing with that cat. Let the cats see each other gradually, first through a glass door and then from a distance in the same room. Give rewards and stop at signs of distress. Avoid any kind of punishment. If none of the above works, medication and hormone treatment are available.

But what in fact was the answer to the question of whether cats prefer living alone or in a group? You may have noticed that I've been 'beating about the bush' and avoiding giving a definitive answer. It just depends. A cat that is allowed outside receives enough stimuli in most cases and doesn't need any other company. An indoor cat that has been socialized from a young age, and feels secure with new, alien situations, can more easily accept and have an exchange with a new cat in the household. It depends on how much stimuli the owner gives the lone cat when they are together.

But what do you do if you've tried to introduce another cat into your home and you realize it's not working? The cats avoid each other or, worse, fight as soon as an opportunity arises. The vet Christopher Pachel, from Oregon, USA, has compiled a list of practical tips from veterinary experience collected from across the world. An early warning sign is that the cats don't interact at all, and the sooner you do something about the situation the better. Use the table above, which lists different kinds of behaviour, to make a diagnosis and decide how to help your cats to get along better.

SCIENTISTS EXPLAIN

How many cats should I have?

- Households with several cats are becoming more common in the Western world.
- According to a study, cats less than two years old in multi-cat households were less stressed than lone cats of that age in a household. Older cats had the same stress levels regardless of the number of cats in a household.
- We should regularly handle and spend time with kittens from two to nine weeks old. It's during this time that the kittens establish social behaviours that endure for the rest of their lives.
- Large individual differences in stress levels between adult cats may be the result of their early nurturing.
- For several cats to get along in a household, they need to know that enough food is available and that they have a safe place to hide and avoid attention.
- Several cats can share a favourite spot in the home, using it at different times during the day.
- A lone cat without other cats in the household can feel contented as long as it gets enough stimuli, either through being outdoors or through daily games with its owner.

Who is Top Cat?

Do a simple experiment: put a box on the floor in front of your cats. The cat that seizes the box first is dominant, and those who don't get access are submissive. Only when the dominant cat leaves the box will the other cats investigate it. After a few days the cats will usually lose interest in the box, but why is it so important to know who is Top Cat and who isn't?

Researchers have long been curious to find out what it is that affects the domestic cat's social organization. The domestic cat went from being a solitary creature to living in a group in less than 10,000 years, which is 'new' in evolutionary terms. Domestic cats form social groups, the core of which consists of 'cat queens' and their offspring. This can be clearly seen in farm cats that live around barns. Male cats don't interact with their offspring; their energy is focused on mating with as many females on heat as possible. Larger and heavier males are more dominant and win more fights than smaller and lighter males. But it's costly to stay on top. Dominant males become fathers to more kittens, but – according to a study led by Eugenia Natoli – they are also more likely to be carriers of a virus that causes feline AIDS, which spreads through bites from other cats.

Just like lions, the domestic cat is sexually dimorphic, that is, there are clear differences between the genders. Males are heavier and have longer canine teeth than females. If only physical

strength were the decisive factor, male cats would always dominate females and their offspring. Such a difference usually becomes clear when it's time for food. Even though female lions –
which hunt in groups more often – are more efficient hunters
than male lions, they have to move aside for the male lion after a
successful hunt. But the domestic cat has unlimited access to food.
Is this the reason why they have a different hierarchical structure?

This was something that an Italian-French research team
led by Roberto Bonanni investigated in an article published in
Animal Behaviour. They followed a group of 13 feral cats living
in a yard surrounded by tall walls in central Rome. The researchers gave food to the cats twice a day for almost a year. They
investigated in what order the cats approached the food bowl,
which was designed in such a way that only one cat could eat
at a time. All behaviour that showed aggression or submission
close to the bowl was noted, and compared later with the cats'
mutual rank and behaviour when no food was available.

Interestingly enough, the results showed a clear difference.
When food was on its way, the females were more aggressive and
assumed a higher rank than many males. And when the kittens
were four to six months old, they got access to the food before both
adult males and females. When no food was served, the conditions
were close to the opposite: almost all the males dominated the
females. There was a clear linear hierarchy, then, where males always held the three top spots and females the three bottom spots.
Regardless of gender, older and heavier cats held a higher rank,
and the higher the rank the cat held the more aggressive it was.

Bonanni and his colleagues don't believe that the domestication of cats can explain this result. They think instead that male

cats don't value food as much as females and young cats because they get enough food anyway. They make an exciting comparison with lions, where the males always have to be in peak physical condition to defend their group of females against competing male lions. A foreign lion male that takes over the group chases the old male away and kills its offspring to bring the female into heat as soon as possible. In the world of the domestic cat, the male can't monopolize all the females. And even if a foreign, dominant male cat comes into the group, the 'old' males remain and can continue to mate in secret with the females. In other words, the researchers believe that the price for male cats to let females and offspring eat first is so small that they can afford it.

It's possible to draw these sorts of parallels to lions with groups of feral cats, which maintain a similar social organization. But what does it look like for the indoor cat, which may be on its own or have the company of only one other cat? Most indoor cats have constant access to food in the form of dry food and there is little risk that foreign cats can gain access to the flat or house. According to earlier studies, neutered indoor cats show a decreased number of aggressive behaviours and more contact-seeking behaviours.

The American researchers Kimberley Barry and Sharon Crowell-Davis were curious to find out whether there were any differences between the genders after all in the number of aggressive or contact-seeking behaviours after neutering. They visited a total of 60 two-cat households and they studied different constellations – male and male, female and female, and male and female – for ten hours in each household. Most of the researchers' expectations came to nothing: the males weren't more aggressive towards females and the females didn't seek more contact with other females. In fact, the opposite was the case: the pairs where the cats spent the most time with each other were those with two males.

The other pattern the researchers noticed was that the number of aggressive behaviours between the cats decreased the longer they had known each other. Interestingly enough, the number of aggressive incidents decreased dramatically after about 10–12 months and stayed at a low level afterwards. This information can be comforting if you've just acquired an additional cat and your cats are fighting each other. Hang in there; there are better times ahead. And if you already have a cat and are going to get another one, it doesn't seem to matter whether you get a cat of the same gender or not – at least if both cats are, or are going to be, neutered.

SCIENTISTS EXPLAIN

Who is Top Cat?

- Domesticated cats create social groups, with 'cat queens' and their offspring at their core. Male cats don't participate in raising their kittens, but focus on trying to mate with as many females as possible.
- Males are 15–40 per cent heavier on average and have longer canine teeth than females.

- A gender's dominance will vary depending on the circumstances. Females are often dominant during food situations but not otherwise.
- Neutered cats in two-cat households don't seem to show any differences between the genders when it comes to contact-seeking or aggressive behaviours.
- Aggressive behaviour declines in frequency over time. After cats have known each other for around 10–12 months, the number of aggressive interactions significantly decreases.

The cat's home area

Few other television programmes about pets have gained as much attention as the BBC production *The Secret Life of Cats*. The programme was a popular water-cooler topic and the programme link was shared thousands of times on Facebook. Finally, we got an insight into what our house cats got up to once they had left their safe homes, until their return many hours later.

What made the programme possible were the technical advances of the digital revolution. In recent years, devices using global positioning systems (GPS) and video cameras have been made ever smaller and lighter. They've now become so small that scientists were able to insert them into cat collars without impeding the cats' movements. With the help of GPS and video recordings, scientists could now both document and explain cats' movements day and night.

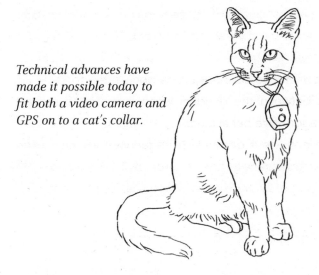

Technical advances have made it possible today to fit both a video camera and GPS on to a cat's collar.

In the television show, it transpired that most of the 50 cats living in a small town in Surrey, England, travelled only a short distance from their home. The cats also moved within fixed home areas. We don't usually talk about territories in the world of the domestic cat because home areas overlap – whereas territories for wildcats don't – and the cat doesn't fully control the borders to its home area – which the owner of a territory does. The television programme showed several cases where two cats divided the same home area between them: one cat patrolled the area during the night and the other during the day. Some cats had even got into the habit of going through the cat flap of another cat's house to steal food. If the cat of the house discovered the thieving cat, they tried to avoid a fight as much as possible and usually had hissing duels until the intruder ran away.

The prosperous and well-groomed house cats in the television pro-gramme had everything they needed and so had no need to hunt to support themselves. They were therefore fairly inactive. But how does a farm or a feral cat move around, either in the countryside or in the outskirts of a city? The Swedish scientist Olof Liberg was a pioneer when he studied cats' movement patterns in the mid-1970s. On foot, on the back of a horse or from a car, Liberg followed between 55 and 72 cats for four years at the military exercise field Revingehed in central Skåne, Sweden. Even when clunky radio col-lars were used for some of the cats, binoculars were the main tool.

A majority of the cats were house cats that were fed regu-larly, but six to eight feral cats were also present in the area. The results showed that males and females had dramatically differ-ent movement patterns. Females had pretty small home areas, centred around the house where they had grown up. They were offered unlimited food, which was a prerequisite for them to feed all their kittens. The males didn't help at all to find food for their kittens. They moved across larger areas than the females, and they moved farther away from home more often once they became sexually mature. The feral female cats had larger home areas than domestic cats and were also more dominant.

Scientists at the University of Illinois, USA, were also curious to see whether movement patterns differed between domestic and feral cats. During 2007 and 2008 they put radio collars on 24 feral cats and 18 domestic cats that congregated in grain stores – in a landscape dominated by grain cultivation. The males had a con-siderably larger home area than the females in this study as well, and feral cats travelled farther than domestic cats. Both scientists and owners were surprised that the domestic cats were so passive.

They slept or stayed in one place most of the time. They moved around less than an hour a day, while feral cats were on the move for three to four hours a day. Because feral cats were forced to find their own food in order to survive, they had to work much harder. Some feral male cats had very large home areas; one mixed-breed male moved across an area of more than 5 square kilometres.

Regardless of whether it was summer or winter, the size of the home area remained the same, but in winter most feral cats stayed closer to humans, within 300 metres of their houses. Scientists offer several explanations for this behaviour. It's easier to seek shelter from bad weather in people's outhouses and barns, and the cats avoid predators such as coyotes and foxes when they stay closer to buildings. They also have more opportunities to find prey because birds and rodents also seek shelter there during winter.

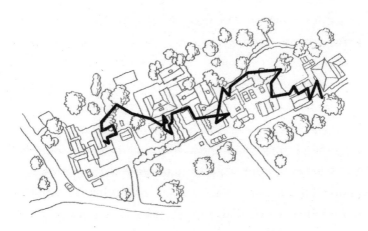

With the help of GPS and video cameras attached to the cats, the researchers were able to track their movements, which revealed that some of them were in the habit of going through the cat flaps of other cats' homes to steal food.

Most feral cats are night creatures, more so than domestic cats. That's why they can avoid close contact with humans and their pets, which are mostly indoors during the cold Illinois winters.

Feral cats appear to be dependent on humans in conditions vastly different from those of the large agricultural plains of Illinois. A Spanish–Portuguese research team captured feral cats in the sq. km Moura/Barrancos, a nature area protected by the EU on the border between Portugal and Spain and home to the Iberian lynx (*Lynx pardinus*), one of the world's rarest cats.

If feral cats and lynx overlap in their areas, there's a risk that feral cats may transmit two dangerous viruses, which can cause feline AIDS and cancer, to the lynx. The scientists put out a number of traps at various distances from traditionally farmed fields, home to a few cows and crops. All the feral cats were captured less than 1,000 metres from a farm. The scientists then put GPS collars on eight of the captured cats. During the mating season, the male cats moved away from the farms, 4 kilometres away on average, but even then they only moved between abandoned farms and not into the 'untouched' wilderness. The researchers believe that the two main reasons for this movement pattern are access to food, which is obviously better close to human homes, and increased protection from foxes. It's clear that feral cats still trust people to provide them with food and shelter. This is good news for the lynx: the risk of them coming into close contact with feral cats and being exposed to their diseases is therefore very small.

Clearly, general movement patterns have been found in the above-mentioned studies. But what is interesting is the large variation between individual cats. Most feral cats cover greater distances than domestic cats, but some domestic cats make extended trips. While most females stay closer to home than males, some females make longer expeditions. It becomes clear that you have to study many different individuals to understand and explain the movement patterns of cats.

Many studies aim to investigate how it's possible to limit the cat's impact on wild or endangered animals. It is then of particular interest to be able to document how and when cats move over time and space. Wild animals with no previous experience of such a competent hunter as the cat could be particularly vulnerable and become easy prey. This 'naive fauna' may be found on small islands where the cat has been introduced, and in untouched natural areas subject to encroachment from a city's expanding suburbs (and its cats). Some examples of such studies can be found in the table on the following page.

Two patterns are clear: the first is that domestic cats move much farther at night than during the day; the second is that they rarely move more than a kilometre away from their home area. This information could work as a guide during urban expansion. One should preferably not build new houses within a kilometre of especially valuable natural areas. Otherwise, there's a risk that domestic cats will make incursions into these natural areas and negatively affect the local fauna (see also the section on the predatory cat, below).

Various studies of potential threats to wildlife from cats

THREATENED PREY	ENVIRONMENT	NUMBER OF CATS WITH A TRACKER	SIZE OF HOME AREA	DISTANCE TRAVELLED FROM HOME	CONCLUSION
Seabirds	The island of Corvo in the Azores archipelago	7 females 15 males	0.2–20 hectares	1,000 metres	The amount of prey didn't affect the movement pattern.
Lizards	Suburbs of two cities on South Island, New Zealand	19 females 15 males	0.2–19 hectares	1,200 metres	They moved farther at night than during the day.
Birds and small mammals	A suburb of Canberra, Australia	4 females 6 males	0.02–28 hectares	900 metres	They moved farther at night than during the day.
Birds and small mammals	A suburb of Reading, England	5 females 15 males	1–4 hectares	400 metres	They moved farther at night than during the day.

SCIENTISTS EXPLAIN

The cat's home area

- The domesticated cat has a home area and doesn't defend territory. Several cats' home areas can overlap and the borders between areas aren't 'defended to the death'.
- Two cats can use the same home area but never meet; one cat is there during the day and the other at night.
- House cats rarely move far from home, which is often in the centre of the home area.
- Domestic cats rarely move more than a kilometre from their home. The most common distance is one or two hundred metres away.
- Females in particular are loyal to their home because this is where food for their young is easily available. Males move away to a larger extent and move across larger areas.
- Non-neutered cats usually have a larger home area than neutered.
- Feral cats are on the move for several hours a day and across a larger area than domestic cats. Some have home areas that extend for several square kilometres.
- Most feral cats will seek out human habitation during the winter for shelter against bad weather, greater protection from large predators such as lynx and fox, and for the availability of food.

The predatory cat

It's a tame and affectionate cat inside the house, but a wild and efficient predator out of doors. The cat's current role as a pampered pet has changed our perception of it and we can often find it difficult to accept its dual personality, despite the fact that we appreciated its hunting abilities during the thousands of years it's been our companion. Even well-nourished domestic cats will kill many small birds and mammals. But how big is the problem? Is it possible to put figures on the number of slain animals?

Several scientists have tried to offer more or less qualified estimates. In the mid-1990s Sören Svensson estimated in the journal *Ornis Svecica* that cats capture round 10 million birds in Sweden every year. This assessment was built on few studies and many assumptions, and Svensson was therefore careful not to overestimate the cat's importance as a predator. But the figures were seized on by the public and are often used in debates as an argument against cats.

Since Svensson's estimate of how much prey cats take, much research has been done and it could be high time to make a new assessment, based on present data, of the number of birds that cats predate in Sweden. A focus on birds is natural since we often see dead birds as a larger problem than dead voles and mice. Other than that, smaller mammals are the most common

prey of domestic cats round the world. Kerrie Anne Loyd compiled information from seven different studies made in Europe, the USA and Australia. Mammals dominated in all studies, with birds the second most common prey. Approximately three-quarters of the prey were mammals while only every fourth prey was a bird. Lizards, snakes, frogs, spiders and insects comprised a very small proportion of the victims.

How many birds does a typical cat take each year, then? American scientists, led by Scott Loss, recently compiled this information in an article in the journal *Nature Communications*. A typical domestic cat in Europe catches 12 birds per year (an average from seven studies), 18 birds per year in the USA (four studies), and in Australia and New Zealand six birds per year (seven studies). I'm only counting on half of all prey being taken home by the cat to show its owner. The estimate of 12 birds per cat doesn't differ much from the numbers that Sören Svensson arrived at (ten birds per cat per year).

Today, however, we have better knowledge of how many domestic cats there are in Sweden. Statistics Sweden (SSW) has produced this information from a survey that was sent out to 20,000 people. There were more than a million cats in my country in 2012 – which is a decrease of about 8 per cent compared to the previous SSW survey from 2006. Simple multiplication tells us that cats in Sweden catch almost 14 million birds per year, a significantly higher figure than the previous, more careful, estimate of 10 million.

The big news in the article in *Nature Communications* was that scientists also tried to estimate the number of feral cats in the USA. They are obviously not as common as domestic cats, but a feral cat captures three times as much prey as a domestic cat. When Scott Loss included these in his calculations, the total sum became horrifying: in the USA, cats kill one to four billion birds every year. In the estimate Svensson made, feral cats weren't included. It's uncertain how many feral cats there are in Sweden, but a figure repeatedly seen in mass media is 100,000. If we use this figure, the sum will have to be adjusted further. Domestic and feral cats in Sweden would catch about 17.5 million birds each year. If only a quarter of all the prey the cat takes are birds and the rest are smaller mammals, we can conclude that cats kill more than 50 million voles and mice every year.

The number of bird pairs is pretty constant year on year. According to the Swedish Ornithological Society, there were about 140 million birds in 2012, or 70 million bird pairs. If these pairs managed to hatch three chicks on average during the summer, there would be a total of 350 million birds in Sweden during the summer. Around 5 per cent of dead birds end up in the jaws of a cat. Of course, we are playing with numbers to a large extent, but it's clear that domestic and feral cats kill a large share of Sweden's birds every year.

But the question is: does the cat's hunting of birds affect the number of birds that survive from year to year? More than 200 million young and old birds don't survive until the next breeding season (because the number of birds in Sweden is constant). The mortality in young birds especially is very high. Many die because they can't find enough food themselves, don't survive the winter migration, get run over by cars, fly into windows, are struck by disease, or are killed by other predators, among many other reasons.

Domestic cats are opportunists: they seize the opportunity when it's offered. They prefer to catch a naive young chick that doesn't manage to fly away or a sick older bird sitting quietly under the bird table in the winter. You might think that the cats' hunting is a good thing in these contexts because these birds were going to die anyway and so they don't have to suffer. But it's not that easy.

Several surveys in Europe show that there is a negative correlation between the amount of prey per cat and the density of cats. Or in other words: when there is a surfeit of cats, the number of birds in the area become so few that it's increasingly difficult for them to catch more. Cats can – at least locally – affect bird populations so much that they decrease or even disappear. The most vulnerable birds to the predatory cat are those that live in city parks and in suburban gardens, birds that search for food on the ground, those that are active at dawn or dusk, birds that have open nests on the ground or in bushes, and those visiting bird tables in the winter. Among these species we find European robins, thrushes, wagtails, pipits, finches, sparrows, siskins and tits. Even birds in the nest can be in danger when a cat lies in wait for the adults to return to the nest to feed their chicks.

To top it all, it may be enough for the cat to disrupt the nest only once for breeding to fail. Colin Bonnington and his colleagues showed this in 2013 in an elegant experiment conducted in Sheffield, England. The researchers allowed a stuffed cat to 'peek' into a blackbird nest where there were eggs or chicks. The distance between cat and the young was 2 metres and, as the control in the experiment, the researchers used a stuffed rabbit. This scenario was repeated for a large number of active blackbird nests, but only once per nest. The researchers concluded

Just one incident of nest disturbance is enough for breeding to fail. In an experiment with a stuffed cat, a blackbird pair with chicks became so upset that nest plunderers like magpies and crows were alerted to their presence. Breeding was more likely to fail with a stuffed cat than when the researchers used a stuffed rabbit as a control.

that the blackbird parents became very distressed and sounded warnings intensively for the cat but not the rabbit. When the blackbirds had older chicks in the nest – and had made a larger investment in feeding the chicks – the parents even attacked the stuffed cat. The parents were still upset nearly two hours after the 'cat' had disappeared, and the chicks in the nest received 30 per cent less food, which would have affected their chances of survival in the long run.

And the drama didn't pass unnoticed. The nests that had received attention from a stuffed cat were plundered by crows more often in the following days than the blackbird nests that had been randomly chosen to be visited by a stuffed rabbit. This is the first time that scientists have shown that just one disturbance to a nest is enough to affect the breeding success of that bird pair. And this disturbance might also affect the size of overall bird populations, since disturbance from cats is likely to be much more common than the cats actually catching prey.

Humans have introduced the domestic cat to a large number of isolated islands. The idea was often to reduce the number of rats, which were also introduced by humans but inadvertently as freeloaders on ships. Unfortunately, it turned out time and again that the opportunistic cat prefers to catch easier prey than rats. The unique fauna on most islands has, during the course of evolution, never encountered such a formidable predator as the cat. Rails, which cannot fly, are often the first birds to be eradicated after the domestic cat arrives. No fewer than 33 species of birds, mammals and reptiles have been rendered extinct by the domestic cat, according to the International Union for Conservation of Nature.

Successful campaigns have been completed on several of the smallest islands where all feral cats have been captured and put down. This was done on the tropical island of Ascension in the South Atlantic between 2001 and 2004. The hundreds of thousands of sooty terns that breed there were easy targets for the introduced cats. To the surprise of the researchers, however, the terns' breeding success didn't improve once the cats disappeared. Rats and mynah birds had taken over the cat's role as predators on eggs and chicks in the tern colonies. The rats literally danced on the table when the cats were gone.

What do we do, then, to limit the negative effect that cats have on wildlife? Eradicating all feral cats within an area seems a little drastic and may well be impossible other than on small, isolated, islands.

The Environment Minister of Australia announced, however, during the summer of 2015 that the government was going to make a serious attempt to eradicate feral cats from parts of this huge continent. There are an estimated 20 million feral cats in Australia, and two million of them will disappear by 2020 to give other threatened species respite and breathing space. There is a widespread view that domestic cats are the main reason why the numbers of many wild animals in Australia are decreasing. Fewer households in Australia have domestic cats: many cat owners probably feel social pressure not to get a new cat.

A bib made of synthetic rubber turned out to be an efficient way of limiting the cat's ability to catch prey (it can't catch them with its front paws). Despite this, few cat owners were prepared to continue using the bib after the experiment.

The Australian researcher Michael Calver wanted to investigate whether there were other methods to limit the domestic cat's opportunities to catch prey. He therefore tested the efficiency of a bib made of neoprene (a synthetic rubber material). In his study of 56 different cats that wore the bib for three weeks, all the cats except one accepted wearing the bib and didn't seem to be much affected by it. The owners collected the prey that the cats brought home while wearing the bib, and for three weeks when the cats didn't wear the bib (either before or after). The bib worked as intended. The number of captured birds was 16 with the bib and 49 without it; corresponding figures for smaller mammals were 59 with the bib and 195 without.

Despite it being an obviously efficient tool, only half of the cat owners were positive about continuing using the bib. Most of the owners had tried other ways to decrease their cats' hunting success. Almost everyone used a collar with a bell, which has been shown in earlier studies to work well. Cats with such collars captured 34 to 48 per cent less prey. Some people scolded the cat when it came home with prey, but that didn't work at all. The only noticeable effect was that the cat ate it in the wild or left it at the hunting site.

The cat mother brings home prey for her kittens to experience hunting. First, the cat mother brings home dead prey, then she brings half-dead prey, and then she finally takes the kittens with her on hunts. Why the lone cat brings home birds and small mammals to us humans is still not clear. But it's not far-fetched to believe the cat either wants to teach us how to become skilled hunters, or to contribute with food to the household. To chastise a cat may only confuse it.

Can it be that some domestic cats are better hunters than others? The vet Id Robertson from Perth, Australia, investigated this through telephone interviews with 458 households with a total of 644 cats (see the table below). Mixed-breed cats caught more prey than pure-bred ones and it wasn't because pure-bred cats spent more time indoors. Neutered cats caught more prey than non-neutered. Cats kept indoors at night caught less prey than those allowed out. If there were one or two cats in the household, each caught more prey than if there were three or four cats in the household. Finally, it turned out that how often the cats were fed and the type of food they received made no difference. The hunting instinct doesn't disappear with a full stomach or luxurious food. However, a study from Chile by Eduardo Silva-Rodriguez and Kathryn

Sieving showed that, if domestic cats are hungry every day, they catch more wild prey.

Results of a study to analyse which cats are the most successful predators

FACTOR	WHAT PROPORTION OF THE CATS CAME HOME WITH PREY?	STATISTICALLY SOUND DIFFERENCE
Gender	Female: 33% Male: 39%	No
Neutered or not	Non-neutered: 24% Neutered: 38%	Yes
Type of cat	Pure-bred: 24% Mixed breed: 38%	Yes
Number of cats in the household	Two or more: 25% One or two: 38%	Yes
Indoors at night	Yes: 28% No: 45%	Yes
Weight	Normal: 34% Overweight: 41%	No
Number of meals per day	One: 37% More than one: 31%	No

SCIENTISTS EXPLAIN

The predatory cat

- Every cat catches around 12 birds each year; they show about half of them to their owner and leave the other half in nature.
- Only a quarter of a cat's prey are birds. The rest are small mammals caught in the wild, such as voles and mice.
- Feral cats catch on average three times more prey than the domestic cat.
- In Sweden, for example, more than a million domestic cats and 100,000 feral cats kill 17.5 million birds and more than 50 million small mammals every year.
- The cat is responsible for about 5 per cent of bird deaths.
- Just one instance of nest disturbance by a cat can be enough to threaten the birds' breeding success.
- Effective ways of limiting a cat's chances of catching prey are a collar with a bell, a neoprene bib and keeping the cat indoors at night.
- Giving a cat plenty of food will not prevent it from hunting wild prey. The hunting instinct will still be there. If the cat goes hungry every day, however, it will catch more prey.
- When your cat comes in with prey, don't scold – but don't praise either. Just dispose of the prey into a rubbish bin or outside without making a fuss.

The mating season

In spring, when the days become longer, unspayed female cats will come on heat. In the northern hemisphere, female cats are usually on heat at the beginning of March, and later on, in April and May, there is another spike where many females are on heat again. It's not unusual for female cats to be on heat all year round.

A female cat's behaviour completely changes at this time: she is more active and more nervous and affectionate. She will tell the neighbourhood's male cats that she is ready to mate by screaming and howling. She will mark her presence with urine here and there, rub her forehead and cheeks against various objects, roll around on the ground, tread with her hind legs, and lie on her front with her behind in the air. This strenuous and gruelling period lasts five to eight days, and the cat often loses a lot of weight during this time. If she doesn't mate successfully, the process will begin again about three weeks later.

The males compete with one another for females on heat. When discouraging growls and hissing don't work, loud conflicts ensue where one party tries to establish his superiority. These fights culminate when the season reaches its peak. We know that there are hierarchies between male cats and that some males dominate others, maybe due to their superior physique or tenacity. But do dominant males get to mate with more females? Or do the females choose their partner based on other criteria than their ability to fight? A French–Italian research team tried to answer these questions by studying two groups of cats, one in central Rome and one in Lyon in east-central France.

The researchers in Rome studied a group of 81 cats living in historic ruins close to a train station. The cats were wholly dependent on humans for food, either through waste food from the nearby market or through friendly people feeding them. As soon as a female came on heat, the researchers studied her for four hours each day over four days. Which cats did she allow to mate with her and which did she reject with aggressive behaviour and no mating? It turned out that dominant males didn't get to mate with more females and that the females weren't too picky about whom they mated with. Seven females mated with several males and showed no preference for any of them. Six other females also mated with several males but allowed certain males to mate with them more often. However, it wasn't the same male that was popular among all six females.

The researchers in Lyon studied a group of 50 cats living in the garden around the Croix-Rousse hospital and fed by the hospital's staff. The study went deeper by using genetic tools to find out whether dominant males were fathers to more young than males of lower rank. The researchers also wondered whether dominant males had less success when all the females were on heat simultaneously, since this could make it more difficult to keep track of covert mating from lower-ranking males. For three years, the researchers studied when the heat period finished for 30 female cats. They also tested the adults and kittens every six months, taking hair samples to determine the parenthood of all the kittens.

It turned out that dominant males were fathers to more young, but only when the females were on heat at different times. When several females are on heat simultaneously, the dominant male spends less time with each female and the chances of successful mating decrease. More than one mating is required for the male to become a father to as many kittens as possible. The reason for this is that ovulation occurs one to two days after the first mating. If several other males mate afterwards, it could result in the kittens of the same litter having different fathers.

When domestic cats live in a group, more often than not the females are on heat at the same time. It doesn't benefit the dominant males but it does provide the females with more advantages. More mating occasions lead to more eggs being fertilized. In around 75 per cent of all litters in city environments, the kitten siblings have two or more fathers. This diversity of genes within the litter is beneficial to the cat's ability to adapt to a life with humans. Another benefit of females of giving birth to young at the same time is that they can divide the burden of raising their young between them. It also reduces the risk of dominant males being aggressive towards kittens when there is uncertainty about paternity. Just as with lions, it's been found that infanticide occurs with domestic cats, that is, dominant males kill kittens that they have not fathered.

It's obvious that males and females have different strategies concerning mating. Which strategy is most successful depends on the environment the cats live in. The studies above were conducted on groups that had plenty of food and shelter. It might look totally different for cats living in the countryside where numbers are fewer and the amount of food is limited. The best strategy in that situation may be for the female to keep close to a dominant male with access to the best territory and the most food for her kittens.

SCIENTISTS EXPLAIN

The mating season

- In the spring, when the days are longer, the mating season starts as female cats come on heat. In northern Europe this often happens at the beginning of March, while in southern Europe it might be as early as January or February.
- Cats are on heat for five to eight days, and then again after three weeks if no mating has occurred.
- Females mate repeatedly to fertilize as many of their eggs as possible.
- Ovulation happens one to two days after the first mating.
- Females will often mate with several males if the opportunity arises.
- Cats that live in groups usually come on heat simultaneously.
- Being on heat is stressful for female cats and can lead to weight loss. You should therefore spay your cat if you don't

wish her to breed. Unfortunately, too many unwanted kittens are born today.

- A short-term alternative to spaying is the contraceptive pill, but it may lead to uterine inflammation and mammary tumours.
- All male cats not used for breeding should also be neutered to allow them to live a calmer life.

2

Your cat's senses

SIGHT, HEARING, TASTE, smell and touch are the five senses all mammals have in common. The cat's sixth sense is its amazing ability to keep its balance. And if it should fall, it will land on all fours. In this chapter, you'll find out how the cat perceives its surroundings.

The cat's memory

One, two, three … where's the ball? You've probably seen the magic trick with three boxes and a ball. With quick hand movements, the magician moves a small ball between three upturned cups. Your task is to then guess which cup the ball is hidden under. Sometimes scientists act like magicians and undertake similar experiments with … a cat. Their purpose is to better understand how a cat's memory works.

A group of German researchers led by Cornelia Kraus published the results from such a study with both cats and dogs in 2014. To make it a little easier for the animals, the researcher used only two boxes instead of three cups and pointed at the box containing a treat reward with an outstretched index finger for a few seconds. The animals participating in the experiment were trained to understand that a treat awaited them if they chose correctly. Cats tired of the researcher's magic tricks more quickly than dogs during this training. If the cats didn't choose correctly – and didn't get the reward – twice or three times in a row, they gave up. Eventually, the researchers managed to train 17 cats and 40 dogs to participate in the 'trick'. The cats and dogs were successful in sniffing out the right box around 70 per cent of the time.

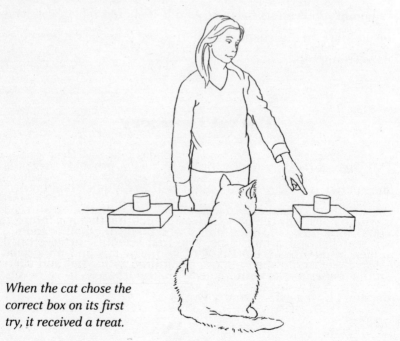

When the cat chose the correct box on its first try, it received a treat.

But it turned out that the dogs were more easily distracted than the cats, which seemed to be able to concentrate better. When the researcher stood right behind the boxes, the dog chose the wrong box more often than when the boxes were a little more than a metre on each side of the researcher. An interpretation of this result is that dogs have less impulse control than cats and that they stare more at the boxes than the outstretched index finger. Another explanation could be that cats in nature often wait patiently for prey, only pouncing when it moves. Could it be that dogs instinctively understand better what we're trying to convey with an outstretched finger, while cats instinctively follow movements? And maybe that's why laser pointers are a more popular toy with cats than dogs. You can entertain your cat for hours as it tries to catch the elusive spot of light moving over the floor and walls.

Cats on the hunt are patient. If the prey is concealed in vegetation, the cat can sit still for a long time waiting for the right opportunity. Sooner or later the mouse will reveal its position with a careless movement. A sudden pounce and the mouse is caught. But how long can a cat sit focused and still remember where it last saw the prey? This is something that has interested researchers for a long time. The first scientific articles on the topic were published almost a hundred years ago and the research field is just as active today.

Two Canadian scientists, Sylvain Fiset and François Doré, recently used the cups and ball trick with boxes and a ball. Instead of two boxes, they used four, on which they had written various geometric symbols. They wanted to find out whether 24 cats remembered where the ball was placed when they first saw it, after waiting behind a closed door before they could start. They also wondered whether the cats used the symbols to find the ball. As in the German study, the cats received a treat when they chose correctly on the first attempt. The researchers also compared the results to how dogs reacted under the same conditions.

The cats were better at finding the ball after ten seconds than after 30 or 60 seconds. But they found the ball more often than randomly, even after 60 seconds behind the closed door. However, the geometrical shapes didn't help the cats to find the ball more easily. If they chose the wrong box on the first attempt, they always continued looking under the next closest. The researchers concluded that the cats remembered the position of the box in the room and not what the box or its surroundings looked like. Dogs remembered the location of the ball better than cats after 30 and 60 seconds. But the researchers were careful to point out that the age and breed of dogs and cats can play a large part in the results. That's why repeated attempts with different breeds and ages are necessary. Only then is it possible to say that a dog's memory is superior to a cat's.

This type of research is incredibly difficult to do well. Cats generally have less need for praise, and lose interest faster than dogs. The conditions for controlled experiments are never particularly natural and the results may tell us more about dogs' and cats' eagerness or otherwise to please than their capacity to remember.

SCIENTISTS EXPLAIN

The cat's memory

- Cats are 'sit-and-wait' hunters that will patiently watch for concealed prey for a long time.
- The cat's instinct to pounce on prey is often triggered by a movement, so unless the intended prey moves the cat will lose interest.
- Researchers don't know for how long the cat can remember where a certain prey is. Few experiments have been conducted in natural conditions.
- Cats have learned to understand humans' visual cues. An outstretched index finger can show them where a reward is. The cat will either follow the movements instinctively or remember from before that a reward will be waiting.

Does your cat listen to you?

Many animals have the ability to recognize their young, their mate and their relatives by hearing their voice, just as humans do. Small individual differences in tone are enough to identify them. There are many examples: female bottlenose dolphins can distinguish from a distance certain whistles or clicks from their young, the common herring gull's young take their first steps out into the world when they hear their parents enticing them from the water below the rocks, and one shout from its young will tell a green monkey that it is in danger from an approaching leopard.

Research shows that many animals can recognize and interpret sounds from different species correctly. The famous elephant researcher Cynthia Moss and her colleagues showed, in an article in the American journal *Proceedings of the National Academy of Sciences,* that elephants listening to recordings of human voices can distinguish a human's gender and age. When family groups of elephants in Amboseli National Park, Kenya, heard recordings of men from the Maasai people saying, 'Look! Over there, a group of elephants are coming', they formed close defensive groups and smelled the air intently. The reactions weren't as intense when they heard recordings of Maasai women or boys.

The researchers also showed that the elephants form defensive groups only when they hear Maasai and not Kamba men; they have obviously learned to recognize different human voices and whether they pose a threat. The Maasai and their grazing animals are regularly in conflict with elephants over access to fresh water and grass, sometimes to the extent that the elephants trample the men to death or the men kill the elephants as a deterrent.

It would seem to be advantageous for domestic animals, just like the elephant, to learn how to understand humans and adapt their behaviour accordingly. This research area has grown exponentially in recent years. Do dogs, cats, horses, pigs and goats understand what we say? Japanese and Italian research teams have examined domestic cats' ability to interpret human speech. They wondered whether domestic cats have learned to pay more attention to their owner's voice than to a stranger's. And once you have the cat's attention, does it listen to *what* you say?

In the Japanese study, 20 cats listened to recordings of five different people calling the cat's name. First, the cat heard its name when three strangers enticed it, then the owner called the cat, and finally another stranger. All of them were instructed to call the name as naturally as possible. The researchers expected the cats to show, in various ways, that they would answer to the first stranger but then quickly lose interest when strangers two and three also called the cat's name. But when the owner called, the cat would react again by either changing the angle of its ears, turning its head, widening its eyes, waving its tail or walking towards the sound. Just as the researchers predicted, the cats got tired quickly but became attentive again when the owner's voice came through the speakers. They either angled their ears or turned their heads towards the sound, but displayed no other differences in behaviour. This shows that they answer to their owner's voice, even if they don't reveal their emotions in the way that dogs do.

But does the cat understand *what* you want to say? An Italian research team made an interesting comparison of how cats and dogs react to a possible threat when their owner is close by. Isabella Merola and her colleagues at the University of Milan used exactly the same trial set-up with 24 cats as in a previous experiment with dogs. Together with their owners, the cats got to familiarize themselves with a room for one minute. After that, the researchers turned on a fan with green plastic ribbons attached to the rotor blades. The cats' reactions to this somewhat odd situation were filmed for careful analysis afterwards. The researchers asked the owners to behave in different ways during three activities. First, they were asked to stand still and stare at the fan for 25 seconds with a neutral expression. This activity was later used as a control for the next two attempts. During activity two, they stood still and with either a happy (half the group) or frightened voice (half the group) looked between the cat and the fan for 25 seconds. Finally, the owner walked up to the fan and spoke in a happy voice or walked away from the fan and spoke in a frightened voice. They also looked between the fan and the cat.

During the first activity, 19 of the cats looked at their owner once after the fan had started, and 13 of them looked at the fan and then their owner several times. They were probably searching for some kind of clue as to how to react. During the next activity there was a bigger difference in how the cats reacted. When the owners spoke in a frightened voice, the cats glanced back and forth between the fan and at a possible escape route located at the side of the room. The cats also started to move away from the fan earlier when the owners showed fear. No such reaction could be seen when the owners spoke in a happy voice. In other words, it's clear that cats can read our emotions and that they adjust their behaviour accordingly.

When the owner spoke with a frightened voice, the cat looked for an escape route from the fan.

Dogs have behaved in the opposite way in similar experiments, that is, they become more immobile when their owner shows fear. Maybe they rely more on their owner to remedy a situation than cats do. The cat's behaviour reflects the fact that it is solitary in the wild and not only a predator but also at risk of becoming prey itself for a larger predator. In other words, it may benefit it to escape at an early stage. Cats didn't follow their owner when he or she walked towards the fan with a happy voice. Dogs, on the other hand, copied their owner's behaviour. When the owner approached the fan with a happy voice, the dog followed obediently.

Several scientists have confirmed the pattern that cats don't fully rely on you even if they listen to you. If cats are facing an unknown and somewhat frightening situation, they don't seek out their owner for comfort, according to a study published in the journal *PLoS ONE* in 2015. The researchers Alice Potter and Daniel Mills showed that cats don't display signs of anxiety when they are separated from us, or exaggerated happiness when we return home. So cats don't seem to have developed emotional ties to humans as strongly as dogs.

But these experiments still show that cats maybe aren't as stoic and independent as they might seem. They recognize their owner's voice and try to interpret our feelings when they face new or threatening situations. That's why it's good to be clear when we communicate with cats. For example, we can explain to the cat with a happy voice that the vacuum cleaner isn't dangerous, and tell the kitten with a frightened voice what could happen if it goes to sleep among the dirty clothes in the washing machine.

 **SCIENTISTS EXPLAIN**

Does your cat listen to you?

- Cats answer to their owner's voice in blind tests.
- In threatening situations, cats try to read their owner's emotions to receive guidance on how to react.
- Cats understand your mood when you speak and adjust their behaviour accordingly. If you use a frightened voice, the cat prefers to run away. If you use a happy voice, it might stay.

- Cats hear sounds at a much higher frequency than humans can manage (65,000 compared to 20,000 Hz). They can therefore hear the sounds of mice and voles that are undetectable to humans.
- Cats can angle their ears independently of each other. This useful adaptation enables them to know what's behind them while also keeping their attention on the prey straight ahead.
- To deter cats from your garden, a scarecrow for cats with ultrasound might work for some, while others don't seem to mind it.

The sounds cats make

Little kittens meow for attention from their mother when they're hungry and want food, or when they're anxious and need comfort. But as the kitten grows, it stops meowing to communicate with its mother or other cats. Instead, it uses a refined language of scents, facial expressions, body language and touch. The adult cat's meow is a language almost exclusively dedicated to humans. Wild and feral cats meow when they're little but more or less stop as adults. They don't have an owner to influence. Hand on heart – do you understand what your cat is trying to tell you? Maybe it's clear from the context when the cat is standing at the door or the food bowl. But it's not always easy, which leads to a frustrated cat and owner.

The sounds a cat makes can be broadly simplified into three groups: sounds from a closed mouth, such as the purring of a satisfied cat; sounds where the mouth is open the whole time, such as the hissing or spitting of a frightened or threatened cat; and, lastly, sounds where the mouth is open at first and then closes gradually, such as the meowing of a cat that is trying to communicate with its owner.

In the UK this sound is written as *meow*, in Germany as *miau*, in France as *miaou*, and in Sweden as *mjau*. Regardless of the language, the sound is written as something that starts with a higher pitch and then goes lower. But in the cat's repertoire there are a dozen different meows that vary in pitch, length and volume.

This is something that piqued Nicholas Nicastros's interest so much that he wrote a doctoral thesis about it. In one of his experiments, 33 research subjects in New York listened to recordings of different meows and then answered questions such as: 'Does the cat sound angry or satisfied?' and 'Does the cat want food or to go outside?' The subjects listened to recordings of cats' meows in the five contexts presented in the table below.

The subjects who had had a cat for longer and socialized with them understood the cat's language better than those less used to cats. They managed to translate about 40 per cent of all meows correctly. Considering that they couldn't see the cats and were just listening to a sound recording, it's an impressive feat. Otherwise, cats often convey their needs clearly through their body language and other behaviours. The meows the test subjects were able to correctly identify were the contact-seeking meow and the meeeooow from a cat experiencing a threat.

What does your cat want to tell you?

	MEOW (BEG-GING)	MEOW (BEG-GING)	MEEEOOOW (FRIGHT-ENED)	MEEEOW (BEGGING)	MEOO-OOW (WORRIED)
TONE	High	High	Low	Rising	Falling
WHAT DOES THE MEOW MEAN?	Hungry	Need for contact	Perceives a threat	Wants to go out	Worry or anxiety
BODY LANGUAGE	Looks alternately towards owner and food bowl	Looks at owner, stomps with legs on the spot	Stares at the threatening object	Looks alternately towards owner and door or window	Wanders back and forth
THE EYES	Open	Open or half-closed	Wide open	Open	Wide open
THE EARS	Up	Up	Back	Up	Down, back
THE TAIL	Up	Up	Down, swishing back and forth	Up	Down, swishing back and forth

All children know that pestering can be beneficial – Mum or Dad will finally give in. Is it the same for cats? If the cat's needs aren't satisfied by a simple meow the first time, maybe it's worth repeating the message: meow – meow – meow – meow (I need/I want to do something immediately)? In a second experiment, Nicastros tested this on 28 new test subjects. It turned out that they understood the message better when they heard repeated meows rather than individual ones. This could explain why cats have become more talkative during the course of evolution the more they've been around humans.

A group of South Korean scientists were curious to see whether calls differed between domestic and feral cats. In their study only female cats were included: 25 feral cats that had been captured for a neutering campaign and 13 domestic cats.

First, the feral cats spent a week in quarantine, where they received daily nursing and food. After that, five scenarios were presented to all the cats. They sat in a cage for three minutes while (1) the owner approached, squatted and spoke kindly to the cat. To the feral cat, the temporary carer approached and spoke kindly, (2) a threatening stranger with a stick approached and made pretend lunges toward the cat's cage, (3) a clothed doll resembling a three-year-old child was pulled on a line towards the cage, (4) an unknown, leashed dog approached the cage and, finally, (5) an unknown, leashed female cat approached the cage. Hardly any cat would feel particularly comfortable with these trials, regardless of whether the cat's origin was feral or domestic.

Sure enough, about 90 per cent of all the sounds the cats made were either growling or hissing. But the most interesting thing was that the domestic cats meowed twice as often as the feral cats, and only when a human approached the cage. The domestic cats' meows were also higher-pitched than the feral cats', whose meow was closer to that of the African wildcat, the ancestor of the domestic cat. It's not too far-fetched to conclude that the domestic cat's short and high-pitched meow is an adaption to communicating better with humans.

It was once believed that only certain felines could purr. Researchers divided them into two groups: smaller felines that could purr but not roar, and larger cats that could roar but not purr. It turned out to be not that straightforward. Several larger cat animals, like the snow leopard, puma and cheetah, can purr but not roar. Today, scientists believe that most felines can purr. The prerequisite for purring is that the muscles in the larynx and diaphragm cooperate so the cat can purr when inhaling and exhaling.

The domestic cat purrs, for example, when you stroke it or when the mother suckles her young. But a purring cat isn't always happy and satisfied. A cat experiencing acute stress or injury can also purr. It could be a way for the cat to calm itself. Today, scientists believe that the low-frequency vibrations from a purring cat can also help to heal injuries more quickly. The vibrations act as massage for sore muscles, and when the cat suffers a broken bone they can increase bone density and speed up the healing process. Today, low-frequency vibrations are being used as pre-emptive treatment for both astronauts and the elderly – people who for various reasons are more sedentary. And maybe even the most sedentary cat purrs to keep its body in shape?

Karen McComb and her colleagues recently showed that domestic cats have different kinds of purrs depending on the situation. Hungry cats purr more loudly and at a higher pitch, and at a frequency on the same level as the scream from a hungry baby. The domestic cat seems to have learned how to communicate with the help of meows and purring to make its owner react quickly to its needs.

 **SCIENTISTS EXPLAIN**

The sounds cats make

- Adult cats mainly use meows when they're trying to tell humans something.
- The meow's message is easier to understand when accompanied by the cat's body language.
- People with previous experience of cats have learned to understand the cat's message just by listening to its meows.

- A cat that has been socialized from young age communicates more by meows and less by hissing and growling.
- Your cat often repeats meows in a series when you don't react the first time. We understand the cat's message better that way.
- If your cat is talking excessively, it could be that it's learned that nagging pays off. To make it stop the habit, you can try to give it food when it is not meowing beside the food bowl or the front door. You should give it plenty of attention when it's silent and doesn't meow as much.

The cat's sense of smell

The cat stops in its tracks when it passes a bush, pushes its head into a low-hanging branch and sniffs intently, lifts its head, opens its mouth as if in a trance and stares straight ahead. It is 'tasting' the scent of a foreign cat's urine with the help of its nose, and its tongue as well. It analyses these scent signals with the help of Jacobson's organ, a centimetre-long duct above the roof of its mouth. This duct is filled to the brim with smelling cells and has two openings, one to the mouth just behind the upper teeth and one to the nose. With this organ, the cat 'reads' the news of its home area. Who passed through here during the night and how did he or she feel? Cats can also do this when they encounter other interesting smells that need closer analysis, but it's primarily associated with scenting urine markings.

The Danish surgeon Ludwig Levin Jacobson was the first person to describe this smell/taste organ scientifically. He discovered it in snakes at the beginning of the nineteenth century. But it took a long time after the discovery for scientists to understand the organ's function. Just like the cat, the snake tastes its surroundings with its tongue and then brings the scent signals to Jacobson's organ for analysis. Many other mammals have this organ as well. Humans lack a similar working organ, however, and our sense of smell is much more limited than the cat's, in which scent signals and pheromones play a much bigger role.

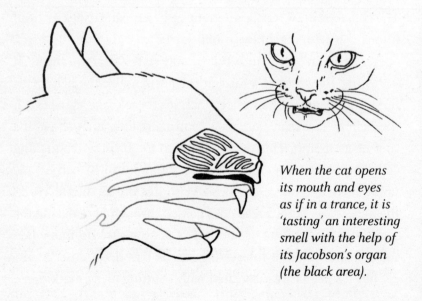

When the cat opens its mouth and eyes as if in a trance, it is 'tasting' an interesting smell with the help of its Jacobson's organ (the black area).

It's not just urine but also a cat's faeces that tell other cats what it is, a Japanese research team revealed recently. Miyabi Nakabayashi and her colleagues conducted an experiment with five different groups of cats. All the cats ate the same dry food before and during the experiment. The scientists gathered the cats' faeces and then one cat at a time entered a room in which three plates of faeces were presented: their own faeces, faeces from a cat in the same group and, finally, faeces from a foreign cat. Each cat had to do the experiment three times with new faeces and where the order of the plates was switched randomly each time.

There were clear differences in how long the cats spent sniffing the different plates. The foreign cat's faeces attracted the most interest. However, the cats sniffed their own stool as long as a familiar cat's. The experiment also showed that the cats got used to foreign cats' faeces: their interest in it wasn't as great on day three.

This experiment can explain why the cat sometimes leaves faeces openly at the edge of its home area. It wants to send a signal to other cats: I live here; don't come close! Especially during the mating season, these markings can help to avoid costly confrontations with unfamiliar cats. The cat covers its faeces much more carefully closer to home, however. The cat doesn't need to signal to other cats to the same extent, and it also doesn't want to risk the faeces spreading diseases to its prey.

Interestingly enough, it has been shown that the cat's prey 'spies on' scent signals between cats. In experiments, it's been revealed that rats can distinguish between different cats just by smelling their collar. Rats that are initially on their guard and hide upon experiencing the scent from a cat collar get used to it quickly and aren't as watchful. If a collar from another cat is presented to the rats, they become vigilant again. This ability to recognize different cats without facing them eye to eye could lead to an extended life for the rat. It knows what threat a known cat poses, but knows nothing about the hunting prowess of an unfamiliar cat.

Cats' urine and faeces contain pheromones that are discharged from glands in mucous membranes in the urinary organs and intestines. But scent signals are also released from other pheromone-producing areas on a cat, which are located on the face, the underside of the paws, around the teats during suckling, and around the genitals and anus. You can get an insight into the cat's wonderful world of scents by studying your cat's behaviour. When the cat is brushing its cheek from chin to ear against your leg, it spreads its face pheromones so that you smell as good as the cat. You are part of the pack.

The cat can also brush its cheek against a doorpost, a screen or similar to orient itself in a room and to feel safe. Pheromones from glands between the pads are secreted in the same way when the cat is clawing. A marker of the home area, this is where the cat feels safe. When your cats have been away from each other for a while, maybe a couple of hours, you can sometimes see that they smell each other's behinds. An important part of a cat's communication is those pheromones in the sacs on each side of the anus. A cat that turns away from you and exposes its behind is a friendly cat that only wants to greet you!

SCIENTISTS EXPLAIN

The cat's sense of smell

- Cats communicate silently with each other through scent signals or pheromones. Long after the sender has left them, these messages remain.
- Pheromones in urine and faeces allow a cat to recognize which other cat has urinated or defecated. A female cat's urine can send signals that show she is ready to mate.
- Sometimes cats don't bury their faeces, which sends a signal to other cats skirting their home area: 'Don't come here!'
- Five areas on a cat's body secrete pheromones: the face, the paws, the teats, the anus and the genitals.
- When a cat brushes its cheek against your leg, it's marking you as a member of its pack.
- You can buy synthetic pheromones specially made to calm stressed cats, at the chemist's and online. Examples of situations that could be stressful for cats are when a new cat is introduced into the home or during a long car journey.

The cat's walking style

The Internet is flooded with video clips of cats making fools of themselves. They misjudge the distance when jumping from the kitchen sink and fall to the floor, or are surprised by a sudden noise and fall off their chair. The clips are often funny but at the same time very unfair. Few other animals have as elegant a walk as cats. Just take the word 'catwalk'. It means a narrow pathway located high above its surroundings. Everyone knows about the catwalk as the elongated stage above the audience on which models stroll back and forth. But construction workers also walk on a catwalk when they balance on beams high above the ground as they construct another floor of a high-rise building. The cat has no fear of heights and will move elegantly on the highest bookshelf and along narrow tree branches high above the ground.

When humans want to move silently, they tiptoe, but we usually walk on the soles of our feet and our toes touch the ground only briefly with each step. Cats are tiptoeing all the time: only the pads under their five toes and the large pad in the centre of the foot touch the ground. And because they retract their claws when they walk, they can move stealthily through the terrain. This is also reflected in the language: someone who creeps like a cat is 'cat-footed'. Toe walkers like dogs and cats can also run very fast. But we all know that there are big differences between how cats and dogs walk: few cats are prepared to go on long walks with their owner and few or no dogs climb trees for fun. Two different research teams have studied in detail why that is and, with the help of video recordings, have investigated how efficiently cats and dogs walk on a flat surface and along a narrow plank.

It probably doesn't come as a surprise to anyone that dogs, which can go on long walks, recycle their kinetic energy more efficiently than cats. A group of American scientists led by Kristin Bishop showed that dogs can recycle about 70 per cent of all their kinetic energy on walks, which makes them twice as efficient as cats. Dogs do so through a rigid gait, which creates an efficient pendulum-like body movement. The cat didn't have to adapt to run long distances during the course of its evolution, and relies more on bursts of energy to make shorter dashes towards prey. None of the cat's walking and stalking techniques are particularly energy saving, and that is why they try to get as close to their prey as possible by moving one paw at a time.

In a French–Spanish study, Eloy Gálvez-López and his colleagues compared how cats and dogs walked along narrow tree branches. The researchers wondered how an expert (the cat) and a non-expert (the dog) would manage this challenge. Different animals have found various solutions to avoid falling from trees. Some have a low centre of gravity, like the tree-dwelling European pine marten with its relatively short legs. Monkeys and opossums have prehensile hands and feet that can grip a whole branch. Sloths have a foolproof solution: they simply hang from the branch. Even though cats and dogs are four-legged animals, it's difficult for them to balance on a tree branch because their paws must be placed one behind the other. On a swaying branch, it becomes even harder for them to keep their balance.

Seven domestic cats and five Belgian sheepdogs were included in the study. In order to make it a bit less challenging for the dogs, their experiment 'branch' was slightly wider (15 cm) than the cats' (3 cm), and the dogs were also given a stable platform at the beginning and end of the branch. The cats and dogs had widely different strategies to keep their balance. The cats didn't change the way they walked on the branch compared to how they walk on the ground. The only difference the researchers could see was that the cats walked somewhat more slowly and crouched down lower on the branch, probably to try to compensate for the swaying of the branch. The dogs did the opposite and *increased* their speed when they stepped on to the branch, and they constantly adjusted their feet in a random way to maintain their balance. This somewhat panicked strategy doesn't pay in the long run; sooner or later the dog will fall to the ground.

But how come cats always land on their feet uninjured in the rare cases when they do lose their balance? The question is simple but the answer is more complicated. In short, the cat has a reflex that helps it determine what is up or down. It probably does this either through sight or by using the balance organ in its inner ear. With its extremely flexible spine, it can then rotate in the air easily so the front part of its body is directed downwards. Although newborn kittens don't have this reflex, they will acquire it after three or four weeks. The cat's tail has no function in the fall. However, the cat avoids over-rotation by pulling in its front legs and stretching out its hind legs. If the fall is from high altitude, the cat stretches out its legs to the side like a flying squirrel, to slow it down. Just before it reaches the ground, it stretches out its forelegs and the cat's unique bone structure

These images show how a falling cat lands on all fours.

works as a shock absorber. The cat's 'shoulders' are extremely mobile because they're not connected to the spine or the chest. So even if the cat doesn't exactly have nine lives, it has some really smart adaptations to survive a fall from a height.

 **SCIENTISTS EXPLAIN**

The cat's walking style

- Cats are toe walkers; only their pads touch the ground when they walk.
- Because they retract their claws when they walk, cats can move almost silently along the ground ('creeping like a cat').
- Cats don't walk for long distances at a time and have a relatively energy-demanding technique. Dogs recycle their kinetic energy twice as well as cats so they can walk for long distances.
- When cats balance on tree branches, they don't change their walking technique compared to walking on the ground. However, they walk slightly more slowly and crouch down low.
- Dogs have a totally different strategy for walking along a tree branch: they increase their speed and place their feet more randomly. Sooner or later, they fall to the ground.
- Cats have a unique skeletal structure and natural reflexes that help them always to land on their feet if they fall.

3

Your cat's behaviour

CATS SCRATCH, URINATE outside the litter box, cough up hairballs, and end up in fights with each other. Life with a cat can sometimes be challenging. It's possible, however, to address many of these problems. But first you need to understand why your cat does these things. This chapter gives you concrete advice to help you restore calm to your home.

Urine markings

Do you think it's difficult to remove the smell of cat urine? That's the point! There are large quantities of the pheromone felinine in a cat's urine, which in turn break down to various sulphuric compositions with the typical smell of cat pee. In the world of cats, the urine markings work like a sort of status update on Facebook: I've checked in today and this is how I feel. The marking should ideally remain in place as long as possible, and that's why it contains various fats (lipids) that prevent the organic compounds from dispersing too quickly.

Many scientists have wanted to investigate what strategies various cats use to increase the longevity of their status update. It's not just the chemical content of the urine that determines how long the message remains, but also where and how the cat urinates. A few years ago I visited the scientist Örjan Johansson, who studies the snow leopard's ecology in an isolated mountain range in the Gobi Desert, Mongolia. The summer there is unbearably hot, the winter is intolerably cold, and there's always a wind blowing. Surely a urine marking can't survive particularly long there?

The snow leopard's strategy turned out to be urinating mainly in the dried-out river valleys that cut through the high mountains. The snow leopard mainly sprayed on rocks shielded from the prevailing wind and with overhangs, so that neither wind nor sun could dry the oil-rich urine too quickly. To make absolutely sure no one accidently missed out on their status update, the snow leopard also scraped up piles of gravel and pebbles in the river valley. This visual signal was then topped off with a shower of urine.

We know considerably less about the urine markings' whys and wherefores in smaller wildcats than in big cats such as the snow leopard, lion and cheetah. The reason for this is that it's difficult to study smaller wildcats in the field because they're

The cat chooses its spot to urine mark with care. Juniper trees are a good choice: they contain antioxidants that don't break down the urine as quickly.

shy and nocturnal. That's why it's not surprising that studies of urine markings in the wildcat and the domestic cat are based on results from big cats in enclosures.

A Spanish research team led by Jordi Ruiz-Olmo studied the urine markings of the European wildcat. The scientists wanted to learn more about what plants the cats urinated on. The wildcats had access to many different shrubs but it turned out that they almost exclusively urinated on juniper bushes. The researchers believe that there are two reasons for these bushes' popularity:

the first is that junipers are visually striking when they're grow-ing in solitary majesty; the second is that the juniper contains high levels of antioxidants, which prevent the urine from break-ing down quickly.

In another study, Hilary Feldman observed 20 cats in an en-closure outside Cambridge, England. She discovered that the males urine marked along the paths they walked and also to some degree the borders of their home areas. They mainly marked eye-catching objects such as tree stumps, protruding branches and tussocks. The males were also particularly at-tracted to urine from females on heat, especially their freshest urine markings.

By analysing similarities and differences in behaviour be-tween 20 different species of cat, among them the domestic cat, researchers have been able to draw conclusions about the function of urine markings. It turns out that marking in males increases dramatically during the mating season in most spe-cies. In other words, the males' markings seemed to work more like an ad on a dating site than a way to assert their territory. Females don't urine mark as often as males, but when they do, it's during the mating season.

It's not just the domestic cat that keeps its tail straight up when it urine marks. Most smaller felines do the same. Scientists believe that it could either be a visual signal to other cats or that it simply occurs automatically during spraying. Every now and again most felines tremble or shake their tail when they urine mark. Maybe this is a way to spread the urine so that the liquid covers a larger area, thus communicating the message better?

SCIENTISTS EXPLAIN

Urine markings

- Cat urine contains fats to make the smell last longer.
- Cats favour urine marking eye-catching objects such as tree stumps, protruding branches, poles, solitary bushes and also the paths they use, for the message to reach as many other cats as possible.
- The same cat will repeatedly mark the same object. It's mainly males who mark, but during the mating season females do, too.
- The urine reveals a cat's state of health or that a female is ready to mate. Urine markings are also used to some degree to mark the borders of a male cat's home area.
- More permanent markings, such as claw marks in trees, or faeces, are probably more commonly used for a home area's borders.
- When cats urinate while shaking their upright tail, it's probably trying to spread its urine over as large an area as possible.

Scratching

All cats scratch with their claws, but at different frequencies and for various reasons. One obvious reason is that the cat is sharpening its claws as well as exercising the muscles in its paws. It's crucial for it to keep the claws in shape for hunting or escaping from an enemy. The scratching can also be a way of getting rid of the outer shell that encloses the growing new claw. The cat usually gnaws the outer shell with its teeth, or it falls off by itself. A third reason can be that the cat is marking its home area. Claw marks send clear signals, not just visual but also via depositing scent trails. Scents are discharged from glands between the pads, which tell other cats that this area is taken. The cats' delicate sense of smell perceives these messages, which we don't.

Cats that scratch the furniture or carpets, even when there are scratching posts nearby, are a big problem for many owners. The scratching can easily become an insurmountable problem, for example if a younger cat wants to challenge older cats in a household for their position in the hierarchy. If a cat is bored, it learns that scratching will get its owner's attention because they'll react immediately when their nice furniture gets scratch marks. Vets are increasingly consulted about what you as a cat owner can do to limit this unwanted behaviour.

Until seven Italian vets investigated the phenomenon more closely, there were only anecdotal observations and no systematic studies. No one knew what normal or abnormal scratching behaviour was. By interviewing a large number of cat owners, they learned more about the whys and wherefores of clawing, enabling them to give better advice to cat owners.

The vets conducted personal interviews with 128 cat owners during their clinic visits. To get as representative a selection as possible, all owners were included, regardless of their cats' sex, age, whether they were outdoor or indoor cats, or whether they lived alone or in a group. The researchers wanted mainly to investigate whether scratching posts were present in the home or not, and to what extent cats used them according to their sex, age, whether they were pure bred or mixed breed, and whether they were outdoor or indoor cats.

It was clearly a good investment for owners to purchase a scratching post or cat tree to have indoors. These devices were often – but not always – used: non-neutered males were the most likely to use them, particularly if they were indoor cats. Non-neutered cats that were allowed outside preferred to claw-mark their home area's borders to avoid potential conflicts with other males; both the claw marks and accompanying scent signals help deter other male cats from intruding on the home area. However, non-neutered females and neutered males and females often used scratching posts and rarely scratched furniture or carpets.

Scratching starts around the age of five weeks, as a kitten starts to play and discover its environment. Once the kitten is separated from its mother, using its claws plays an important role in its new surroundings. It's a way for the kitten to determine in which areas it can feel safe and in which areas it should be on its guard. However, no cat will use a scratching post that is poorly placed or made from the wrong material. And it can be very difficult to break the habit once a cat has started to claw at a certain piece of furniture or section of carpet. After all, the cat likes to return to 'the scene of the crime' to strengthen its scent trail.

Vets from Cornell University in New York have compiled several strategies to get to grips with the unwanted scratching of furniture and carpets, despite the presence of a scratching post in the home. Does your cat prefer to scratch vertical surfaces, like curtains or the back of furniture, or horizontal surfaces, like carpets? Does it scratch hard or soft fabric? Cats differ in their preferences, which can give you a good indication of what your cat's scratching post should look like and where it should be placed.

Temporarily move away the item of furniture or rug and place the scratching post there instead. You can then gradually move the post to a more suitable place, and then after a while move the furniture or rug back. If the cat still continues to scratch in the wrong place, you can try spraying a strong perfume on the area or build a tower of plastic cups in front of it, which will frighten the cat when it topples the tower.

Remember that punishments like scolding or squirting water from a spray bottle don't work. They only teach your cat to scratch when you're not there. However, praise works brilliantly when the cat behaves correctly. Finally, you can limit the damage by keeping claws short with the help of nail clippers.

 **SCIENTISTS EXPLAIN**

Scratching

- Cats have a natural urge to scratch with their claws, to sharpen them, to exercise their paw muscles and to mark their home area through visual (claw) marks and scent signals.
- Non-neutered males that aren't allowed outside are the most frequent users of scratching posts.
- Studying your cat's behaviour will help you decide on the best position and design for a scratching post.

Tail in the air

The wildcat is a lone hunter; adult wildcats don't form social groups. By contrast, the domestic cat has in many different ways been forced to adapt to living in a group. Every day our cats meet their own kind, and to avoid costly confrontations they have had to develop a body language to clearly signal their mood or rank within the group.

One of these social signals between cats is the tail in the air. You've probably seen it at home if you have several cats. Two adult cats have been away from each other for a while. Maybe one of them has been out while the other stayed indoors. When they meet again, one cat lifts its tail in greeting, keeping it vertical with the tip of the tail pointing straight towards the other cat. They may follow this by smelling each other nose to nose, where the greeting cat keeps its head lower and its ears angled back. This behaviour, its meaning and origin, is something that has interested ethologists (scientists who study animal behaviour) for a long time.

Two Italian ethologists, Simona Cafozzo and Eugenia Natoli, studied a group of domestic cats living freely in a backyard in Rome. The yard was partly overgrown and surrounded by tall walls. The cats were four neutered males and females and a young, non-neutered male. Some were domesticated enough to accept being petted. The scientists studied the cats' behaviours for 400 hours over a nine-month period. To investigate the ranking within the group, they studied the outcomes of interactions that showed aggression or submission. They then compared the ranking within the group with how the cats greeted each other.

Two of the adult males were highest in rank within the group, while the young male had the lowest rank. Cats of higher rank seldom showed the tail-in-the-air signal when meeting individuals of lower rank. Conversely, individuals of low rank almost always gave this signal when encountering individuals of higher rank. The ethologists also found an interesting gender difference in the way the cats greeted each other. Males greeted more often nose to nose, while females preferred to lift their tail in the air or brush their bodies against each other.

This and several other studies show that a sender who always uses the tail-in-the-air behaviour gives a clear signal to the receiver: I'm friendly and I know that your rank in the group

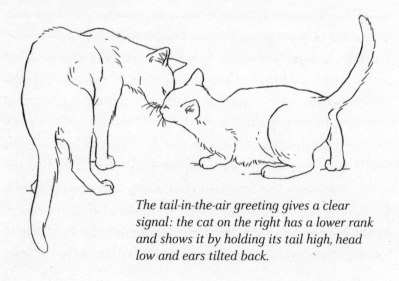

The tail-in-the-air greeting gives a clear signal: the cat on the right has a lower rank and shows it by holding its tail high, head low and ears tilted back.

is higher. If the receiver chooses to respond to the sender by also lifting its tail, they are likely to complete the ritual with a nose-to-nose greeting and by brushing their bodies against each other. Most often, however, the greeting phase stops after the first tail lifting.

The tail-in-the-air greeting has been observed only in one other feline: the lion. The lion and the domestic cat are the only cats that live in social groups. Lions live in groups consisting of closely related females and their young, as well as some unrelated males. Farm cats living in the countryside have a social structure not very different from lions in the savannah: closely related females and their offspring create loosely connected groups round the sources of food offered by humans.

Evidently, the tail-in-the-air signal has developed separately in the lion and the domestic cat, and we can only speculate on its origin. Cafozzo and Natoli present three hypotheses. The first is that when cats urinate they lift their tail in the air, but because this behaviour isn't supposed to signal anything to a receiver, they seem to disregard it immediately. The two other hypotheses seem more reasonable because they're based on signals that are already used in other contexts. The first is a ritualized sexual behaviour by the female prior to mating, which includes both brushing with the body and lifting the tail (as described in the classic book *The Serengeti Lion* by George B. Schaller). Finally, perhaps the most probable explanation is that when a kitten wants to suckle its mother, it approaches with a lifted tail and butts its forehead first and then its head against her chin. Kittens also show this behaviour towards adult cats, and it's not particularly far-fetched to suggest that this 'childish' behaviour has been retained in the domestic cat as a way of suppressing aggressive behaviour in others and displaying their lower rank. In fact, some domestic cats use chin butting and the raised tail towards their owners as a way of showing their lower rank within the family.

SCIENTISTS EXPLAIN

Tail in the air

- The tail-in-the-air greeting has been observed in only one other feline: the lion. Only two cat felines create social groups: the lion and the domestic cat.
- The domestic cat has in various ways been forced to adapt into living in a group.
- Cats of lower rank give the tail-in-the-air signal to greet cats of higher rank. By this means that both cats confirm their position in the group and this can avoid costly confrontations.
- When a kitten wants to suckle, it approaches its mother with a lifted tail. Maybe adult cats have retained this 'childish' behaviour as a signal to show their rank within the group.

Where your cat wants to be stroked

When you're reading a good book with a purring cat on your lap, you probably feel great. You stroke the cat gently, but suddenly you receive a light bite or an annoyed tail movement. What happened? Perhaps you stroked it a little too close to the base of its tail. Unlike dogs, most cats don't like being stroked there. But you obviously want the cat to feel good, so where is the spot on its body where the cat enjoys being stroked the most?

Your curiosity can now be satisfied: two investigations, in England and New Zealand, examined cats' responses when they were stroked on different parts of the body. Firstly, the researchers were curious about three areas where the cat discharges scents through superficial glands: at the base of the tail, at the temples between eyes and ears, and from the chin to the corner of the mouth. When your cat brushes against your leg or hand, it is marking you with scents from its scent glands without you noticing. You then smell just like the cat.

In the English experiment the researchers studied 34 cats in their homes. Firstly, they got acquainted with the cats for 15 minutes. After that, they stroked eight parts of the cat's body where the owner usually stroked. Apart from the three areas where the cat has its scent glands, they also stroked the top of the head, the neck, the back, the chest and the throat. Only the index and middle finger were used and the scientists stroked for 15 seconds. The procedure was repeated the next day, but this time it was the owner doing the stroking. The scientists videotaped everything and then categorized the behaviours from a predetermined list, an ethogram (see the table below).

This table shows all the behaviours the English scientists had agreed on in advance when assessing responses when they stroked the cats. A minus (–) means the behaviour was assessed as aggressive or avoiding behaviour, while a plus (+) was assessed as a contact-seeking behaviour.

BEHAVIOUR	MEANING	DESCRIPTION OF BEHAVIOUR
Bites	–	Opens the mouth and uses teeth to touch the object.
Licks Lips	–	Puts out tongue to lick lips.
Air Bites	–	Opens the mouth and quickly closes it again.
Yawns	+	Opens the mouth slowly and completely.
Grooms Itself	+	Uses tongue to lick its fur.
Grooms Others	+	Uses tongue to lick a human.
Blinks	+	Opens and closes eyelids slowly.
Closes Eyes	+	Closes eyes for more than 3 seconds.
Draws Ears Back	–	Keeps ears back along the body.
Twitches Ears	–	One or both ears twitch as a response to stimuli.
Pushes Head	+	Pushes head or brushes face against a human.
Turns Away Head	–	Turns head away from a human.
Turns Head Quickly Towards	–	Quickly moves head towards a human.
Turns Head Slowly Towards	+	Slowly moves head towards a human.

Brushes Head Against	+	Brushes head against an object or the ground.
Sniffs A Human	+	Sniffs or smells a human.
Sniffs The Air	+	Sniffs an object 'in the air'.
Lifts Tail Up	+	Holds the tail straight but with the tip bent.
Hits With Tail	–	Holds the tail straight but with the tip waving back and forth.
Trembles With Tail	–	Holds the tail upright and quivering from base to tip.
Moves Tail Back And Forth	–	Moves the tail back and forth when lying or sitting.
Points Tail Straight Up	+	Points the tail straight up to the sky.
Tail Waves To And Fro	+	Moves the tail rhythmically back and forth.
Tail Embraces Body	+	Curves the tail round the body when sitting or lying.
Paw Touches	+	Stretches the front paw to pat or touch an object.
Paw Hits	–	Hits an object or human with the front paws, claws out.
Paws Tread	+	The paws knead the ground with claws out or in.

The shaded areas of the body are where the cat exudes scent from superficial glands.

The cats were free to leave whenever they wanted if they got tired of the stroking. And it came as no surprise that only 16 of the 34 cats allowed themselves to be stroked in all eight places. More surprising was that the cats showed more aggressive and avoiding behaviours towards their owners than towards the researchers. One explanation the scientists put forward was that the cat more easily grew tired of its owner when their behaviour was unexpected. And curiosity towards a stranger might have made the cats more tolerant of the researchers' behaviour.

Regardless of who did the stroking, it was clear that the cats didn't want to be touched close to the base of their tail. They preferred being stroked on their head, particularly in the two areas where the cat has scent glands: on the temples and between chin and cheek. It's also here where cats focus their efforts when they groom each other. When you stroke the cat in your lap, you should therefore communicate in the cat's preferred way and focus on its head. Females on heat, however, do enjoy being petted close to their tail, but it's probably a different form of pleasure they are seeking.

Only nine cats were studied in the New Zealand experiment, and the scientists stroked only the areas of their body with scent glands. The scientists categorized a smaller number of behaviours than the English study, but the results were completely consistent between the studies.

SCIENTISTS EXPLAIN

Where your cat wants to be stroked

- Cats have superficial scent glands by their temples and between their chin and cheek. These areas are where the cat prefers to be stroked because scent is released which makes you smell homely to the cat.
- Avoid petting around the tail where the cat also has scent glands. Only female cats on heat like it.
- If you already have a cat and are going to introduce another into the household, rub a clothed toy or a blanket on the temple or chin of the new cat and give it to the 'old' cat, and vice versa, before they meet, to get them used to each other's scent.

Hairballs

Cats are clean animals. They lick themselves or each other during a large proportion of their waking hours. Because their rough tongue is covered with little barbs, it's not surprising that cats swallow large amounts of hair every day. This is usually not a problem; the hairs pass through the intestines undigested and out with the faeces. But when so much hair accumulates that it can't pass through the duodenum, the cat must cough up a hairball.

Owls and many other birds regurgitate balls of fur and feathers, and bones as well. It's a necessary part of their digestion. The bird can only eat again once the pellet has been ejected. Cats don't have the same physiological requirement; if they did, they would produce hairballs every day. Fortunately, cat hairballs are a less common phenomenon. Many cat owners think they are normal and never ask their vet for advice. Surprisingly few scientists have spent time studying the phenomenon closely, at least until recently when the vet Martha Cannon from England published a careful review of cat hairballs.

How often do cats vomit hairballs? It's a seemingly simple question, but the truth is that we have hardly any information about it. That's why Cannon asked cat owners who visited her clinic for vaccinations. Cats with known stomach, intestinal or skin problems weren't included in the survey because they're expected to have more problems with hairballs than healthy cats. Hairballs

were uncommon in healthy short-haired cats; only 20 per cent of these cats vomited two hair balls or more per year, compared to 55 per cent of long-haired cats. More than half of the short-haired cats had, as far as the owners were aware, never vomited a hairball.

Hairballs are common in long-haired cats and they don't necessarily mean that anything is wrong. In short-haired cats hairballs could mean a chronic intestinal disease – for example, intolerance to certain kinds of food – where symptoms mainly appear after the cat has eaten. Hairballs, diarrhoea and frequent ingestion of grass to induce vomiting are all signs that something may be wrong with its stomach. The most common reasons for a cat to swallow too much hair, however, are flea infestations and skin diseases, which make the cat lick itself an abnormal amount. Anxiety and pain can also lead to excessive licking.

So how can you help your cat avoid hairballs? You can partly overcome the problem by changing the cat's diet, although there is no published scientific evidence that special foods to combat hairballs work, despite their being marketed as scientific diets. It's also uncertain whether a 'natural' diet consisting of raw minced meat or meat on the bone helps to reduce the incidence of hairballs – or that it gives the cat healthier teeth and a shinier coat. Feeding your cat little and often can help its gastrointestinal tract to digest the food more easily so that the hair comes out naturally. Adding a few drops of liquid paraffin to your cat's food can also help its digestion and prevent constipation.

A simple solution that guarantees results is to reduce the amount of hair the cat can ingest. Brushing your cat daily is a way forward and, for recurring problems in long-haired cats, a 'lion cut' (where all the fur except on the head, legs and tail is cut short) could be a solution. If problems remain, consult your vet, who will examine your cat to see whether an underlying disease is causing the hairballs. If that's not the case and none of the above advice helps, the vet can prescribe medicine to alleviate the discomfort of hairballs, even if it doesn't prevent them.

 **SCIENTISTS EXPLAIN**

Hairballs

- Cats naturally ingest large quantities of hair every day. Coughing up a hairball once in a while doesn't necessarily indicate a problem.
- Hairballs are twice as common in long-haired as short-haired cats.
- If your short-haired cat regularly vomits hairballs, it may mean that it is licking itself excessively due to a flea infestation or skin disease, or that its gastrointestinal tract isn't working as it should.
- The easiest way of getting to grips with hairballs is to reduce the amount of hair your cat ingests by brushing it regularly.
- Giving your cat smaller portions of food can often help digestion, and if that doesn't work you could add a few drops of paraffin oil to the food to reduce constipation.
- There are also special diets for hairballs which could have an effect, although there is as yet no published scientific evidence for this.

95

Grooming

Gorillas, horses, parrots and cats are examples of species that carry out social grooming in pairs. The grooming's function is partly to remove dirt and parasites, and partly social to strengthen friendship bonds and decrease conflict-filled situations between individuals. Humans undertake social grooming when we scratch each other's backs or remove lice from our children's hair.

The key words for cats living in groups are tolerance and avoidance. The cats may divide up their spaces and sleeping spots between them, and socialize with their owner at different times of day. This division of time and space can reduce the number of conflicts. Grooming has an especially important function for cats living in groups. It's a way for the cats to avoid open conflicts. Scientists have wanted to learn more about this social interaction, particularly in contexts when the cats don't have the opportunity to be apart from each other at any time of day, as well as cats that never go outside or that live in cat homes.

To learn more about cat grooming, we first need to find out how cats lick their own coat. The researchers Robert Eckstein and Benjamin Hart from California did two experiments to understand more about the whys and wherefores. All the 11 cats in the study were free from parasites, since the presence of cat fleas and other parasites will make a cat lick itself more often.

First, the researchers described the cats' activities for two days, from six in the morning until six in the evening. Each cat had a room to itself and everything was video-recorded for careful analysis afterwards. The cats mostly licked their face with the help of their paws and thereafter, to a lesser extent, their hind legs, the front part of their body, neck and chest, genitals, rear part of the body, and finally the tail. They usually started with the face and systematically went through each body part towards the tail. The cats would often lick their coat thoroughly after an extended period of sleep.

In the second experiment, nine cats wore a cone round their head for three days. The cats could do everything they needed except lick themselves. After that, the researchers removed the funnel and compared how much they licked themselves with a control group that wore only a collar. During the first 12-hour period, it seemed as if the cats with the cone had a pent-up need to lick themselves considerably more often than the control group. However, there was no difference during the second 12-hour period. Together with previously conducted physiological studies, these experiments seem to suggest that cats without parasites lick their coat out of habit rather than because their coat is dirty. Cats obviously lick themselves when they're dirty, but considering the disproportionately long time they spend on this activity, it seems that the inherent instinct to lick themselves is strong.

How does it work, then, when two cats groom each other? In a series of articles, the Dutchman Ruud van den Bos got to the bottom of this question. He studied 24 cats that had known each other since they were kittens. Some of them were closely related; others weren't. Regardless of gender, they were all neutered.

The cats had been studied before and a rough division of rank (high, middle, low) had been made. Van den Bos studied the interactions of pairs during a six-month period. The licking cat usually stood up and the cat being licked lay down, and usually the neck was licked. The licking was usually not mutual, and in a third of the cases it concluded with the licking cat getting angry with the recipient cat – hissing, growling or flicking its tail in annoyance. In more than 90 per cent of the cases, it was a male who initiated the grooming. Individuals of higher rank licked the ones of lower rank. Closely related cats didn't lick each other more than unrelated cats.

Based on these results, Ruud van den Bos concluded that cats don't lick to clean each other. They also don't lick as a way to ingratiate themselves with individuals, according to the motto 'lick upwards, kick downwards'. He suggests instead that grooming is a way of releasing tension between cats. The licking closely resembles a pretend attack where the dominant cat often displays aggressive behaviour and mostly licks the neck, a part of the body that cats tend to attack during a fight.

Sometimes grooming isn't enough to release tension within a group of cats. Two cats have a brief spat, and shortly afterwards they retreat to their own corner, nervously licking their nose and body. These are typical reactions after the surge of stress that the fight released. Van den Bos showed in his studies that these behaviours ceased a few minutes after the fight. However, if a cat experiences long-term stress or is nervous, licking could become a problem. A cat licking away patches of fur from its coat can obviously be due to various diseases or allergies, but the reason can also be psychological, such as the cat never being able to relax.

SCIENTISTS EXPLAIN

Grooming

- Cats groom themselves by licking first their face and then moving systematically down the body towards the tail.
- Cats lick themselves particularly carefully after an extended period of sleep.
- Cats obviously lick themselves when they're dirty, but also instinctively lick themselves regularly throughout the day.
- When cats lick each other, it's not to clean or to befriend the other cat. Rather, it's a way for cats to ease tension and decrease aggression within the group.
- Cats lick themselves intently after a fight. This reaction is the way they calm themselves down.
- A cat exposed to prolonged stress may lick away patches of fur from its coat. Seek advice from a vet to ensure that it's not a disease causing this behaviour. After that, you can think about changing something at home to make your cat feel more relaxed. You can buy synthetic pheromones to calm cats from your vet or chemist.

4

Your cat's temperament

HOW DO YOU get a friendly cat? Is it just inheritance or can upbringing affect how sociable a cat becomes as an adult? In this chapter you will learn more about how to socialize your cat to make it feel safe. You will also be given advice on how to get to grips with aggressive behaviour so that both you and the cat can enjoy a peaceful home.

A secure upbringing

You want a friendly and sociable cat that likes being with you, your family, your friends and any other household pets you may have. You want a cat that greets you and your family with raised tail and brushes against your legs, and that purrs if you pick it up, kneads its paws and pushes its face against you when you stroke it, and maybe even drools with contentment. A cat like this obviously feels happy, and your friends also get to take part in this pleasurable experience. A cat that prefers to withdraw rather than greet – and maybe hide somewhere where it can avoid eye contact – is an uneasy cat that feels uncomfortable with domestic life. But how do you get a secure and sociable cat?

This issue has interested scientists for a long time. And the question always asked in these studies is whether it's inheritance or environment that creates social behaviours. If it's the environment that is decisive, then the follow-up questions are: at what age, and what can we do to make our cat feel as secure as possible?

Sandra McCune from the University of Cambridge in England wanted to investigate whether inherited traits from the father influenced how sociable a cat became later in life. The genes from the mother's side also matter but this is more difficult to investigate because kittens usually spend their first months solely with their mother. To then determine which of their behaviours are created by maternal genes and which by environment is nigh on impossible.

McCune designed an ingenious experiment to determine the comparative significance of inheritance and environment. Two tom cats were fathers to six litters each; one of the fathers showed all the signs of being unfriendly and insecure while the other was sociable and assured. Half of the unfriendly father's litters became socialized between two and 12 weeks. A carer visited them every weekday, and she petted and spoke kindly to the kittens for an hour while they sat on her lap. The other half had minimal contact with the carer, who only came in to give food and clean the litter. The same thing happened with the sociable father's kittens: half were socialized and half not.

At the age of one year, all the cats participated in three different experiments. First, a carer who was known to the cats sat on a chair in the middle of the room, then a stranger sat on the chair, and in the last experiment the chair was replaced by a wooden box with two openings. All the cats' behaviours were documented by a scientist concealed behind a mirrored window (like the one you see in police interview rooms in films).

Of the four different groups, two stood out in all the behavioural tests: the group that had a friendly father and had been socialized when young (behaviours: greeted immediately, brushed against the person, kneaded with the paws); and the group that had the unsociable father and minimal contact with people when young (behaviours: hissed, hid). The cats in the other two groups were somewhere in between in all the tests. The results were the same regardless of whether or not the cats already knew the person who came into the room. So it's not actually inheritance *or* environment, but inheritance *and* environment that determine which social behaviours cats display as adults.

The experiment with the wooden box gave an interesting clue to why genetics can be an important factor. It turned out that it didn't matter at all if the cats had been socialized when they were young. The only thing that determined whether the cats were curious and entered the box was if they had a friendly father. McCune believes that what scientists call friendliness also includes characteristics such as bravery and curiosity to explore new situations. And it was that inheritance from the friendly father that made them go into the wooden box, while the young from the unfriendly father stared suspiciously at it. Finally, it was concluded that the socialization of kittens at a young age (environmental factors) enables them to get used to being with humans, but not to be bold and daring in unknown situations. Hereditary factors play a bigger part there.

When and how should you best socialize your cat to make it secure and friendly as an adult? Sarah Lowe and John Bradshaw from the University of Southampton in England have studied in detail from what age you should start socializing kittens. The answer to their investigation was clear: the earlier the better. Start at the age of two weeks. If you wait until the kittens are older than seven weeks, the socialization with humans won't be as effective. It's also important to keep socializing the cat even between eight and 16 weeks old. That's when the socialization is 'fine-tuned', and the cat learns to handle not only known people but also strangers in new situations. Having lively dinner parties when your kitten is three to four months old – where all the guests are cuddling the kitten – maybe isn't such a bad idea!

Studies have shown that adult cats are less afraid of new people if several people handled it when it was little. And you should ideally handle it for a long time every day; cuddling and playing with your kitten for at least 45 minutes a day produces a friendlier and more secure adult cat than one cuddled and played with for only 15 minutes a day.

SCIENTISTS EXPLAIN

A secure upbringing

- Play frequently with your kitten from two weeks until it's four months old. This socialization produces a friendlier, more secure cat, which makes a happier adult.
- The more that people play with the cat the better. However, don't forget that cats also need a lot of sleep, so don't interrupt sleeping kittens. And if the cat seems stressed or frightened when playing, it's obviously better to take it easy.
- Cuddle and play with your kitten for at least 45 minutes a day rather than 15, but stop immediately if the cat clearly shows it can't or doesn't want to continue.
- It's not just the environment where the cat grew up that influences it as an adult. Genetic factors can also determine whether a cat is brave and curious, which in many cases can be interpreted as friendliness.

Cats' charisma

There's no uncertainty whatsoever that cats are great personalities. The charisma cats radiate competes with that of the biggest movie stars. In fact, cats such as Nala, Grumpy Cat and Lil BUB have millions of followers on Instagram, more than most human celebrities. More than two million cat videos were uploaded to YouTube in 2014 alone. And no other category on YouTube measures up to the 26 billion views that cat videos have had so far. All this and more can be read about on internetmuseum.se, where the cats-on-the-Internet phenomenon has been gifted its own separate exhibition. But why do cats dominate the Internet?

The researcher Radha O'Meara from New Zealand believes that their popularity has to with cats being mysterious, dignified and untameable. That's why it's unexpected when a cat messes up and we laugh at how aggrieved it looks afterwards. We transfer our own emotions on to the cat, something psychologists call projection. Deep down we probably know that Grumpy Cat wasn't particularly grumpy or tetchy.

In the journal *Psychological Reports*, Christina Lee and her colleagues from Missouri, USA, let the owners of 196 cats assess their cats' personality. The scientists wanted to investigate whether it was possible to describe cats' personalities in the way that psychologists do with humans. According to the 'five-factor theory', humans have universal traits in their personality that are neither culture- nor situation-dependent: openness to experience, conscientiousness, extraversion (outgoing/energetic vs solitary/reserved), agreeableness, and neuroticism (sensitive/nervous vs secure/confident).

Lee and her colleagues wanted to find out whether the cat's gender and age influenced its personality. The cat owners ranked 12 different personality traits from 1 (don't agree at all) to 5 (completely agree) according to how they corresponded with their cats. Four different groups could be distinguished after the statistical treatment of the material. The first group had common traits such as wise, curious and social, while the second had sensitive, agreeable and protective. The third had aggressive and angry traits and the fourth had reclusive ones.

The older the cats in the study were, the less their owners perceived them as sociable, playful or curious. However, the gender of the cat had no influence on the results, which surprised the scientists. They expected more male cats to belong to the third group with aggressive and angry traits. Because the scientists didn't know how many of the cats were neutered, they couldn't say for certain what role gender played in the cat's behaviour.

In 2013, Marieke Gartner and Alexander Weiss from Edinburgh, Scotland, evaluated all 20 articles that have been published so far about the domestic cat's personality. The personality traits that dominated most articles were that cats were social, dominating and curious. They also found that the cats' ages influenced personality, just as Christina Lee and her colleagues had shown. Surprisingly enough, no study has investigated in detail what significance neutering had for the cat's personality, or whether there are differences in personality between pure-bred and mixed breeds.

Gartner and her colleagues showed, in an article from 2014, that the domestic cat's personality differs surprisingly little from that which wild felines display. They used the same protocol to assess animals in captivity: the snow leopard, tree leopard, lion, European wildcat and domestic cat. All cat animals displayed common traits, such as dominance, neuroticism and impulsiveness.

Research on cats' personality has a bright future. Maybe we'll find cats who are grumpy and tetchy 'for real'. Grumpy Cat may have looked grumpy, but, according to her owner, Tabatha

Bundesen, the reason for that look wasn't a personality trait the cat suffered from, but achondroplasia (dwarfism). But Tabatha isn't particularly sad because the sale of books, toys, clothes and cat food depicting Grumpy Cat has generated 50 million US dollars in two years. That's more than the Swedish footballer Zlatan Ibrahimović earned in the same period. That's how big an impact cats on the Internet can have!

SCIENTISTS EXPLAIN

Cats' charisma

- Just like humans, domestic cats seem to have universal behaviour traits that are unconnected to a specific situation.
- Cats are usually described as social, dominating and curious by their owners. But cats may also be sensitive, friendly and protective. A third group can be described as aggressive and angry, and a fourth as reclusive.
- The older cats are, the less sociable and curious their owners perceive them to be.
- Neither its gender nor its breed seem to make a difference to a cat's personality traits.
- More research is needed to find out how neutering affects a cat's personality.

Aggressive cats

Anyone who has ever petted or played with a cat for a little too long has probably experienced it; without warning, the cat hisses and bites you hard on the hand. In most cases, the cat has already signalled that it's had enough. But it's not always easy to notice the irritated quiver of the tail tip or the tilted-back ears. We might be so preoccupied with the play that we continue even when the cat has told us to stop.

Compared to a bite from an aggressive dog, we don't usually see the bite from a cat as a serious problem because the wound is often superficial. Despite that, cat owners are increasingly visiting the vet to get to grips with their aggressive cats. And if the treatment the vet suggests doesn't help, the cats are often left at a cat shelter. The reason for cats being left at shelters in the USA in 15 per cent of cases is that they're aggressive towards humans, and in 12 per cent of cases it's because of their aggression towards other cats.

Can we predict which cats are at risk of becoming aggressive towards humans? A Spanish research team led by Marta Amat made an interesting comparison between two groups of cat owners who visited the vet: the first group sought advice because their cats were aggressive and the other group was making a routine visit for vaccination or a health check (no behavioural problems). It turned out that the combative cats were more often indoor cats, came from households with only one cat, had been bought from a pet shop, and were not neutered.

Earlier studies have also shown that females are more aggressive than males. The situations that mainly triggered the cat's aggression towards humans were play and petting. Because the cats showed their aggression in connection to play, the scientists concluded that lone cats – particularly those that aren't allowed outside – had an unmet need to play and their needs weren't being fully met by their owner. The share of indoor cats was 78 per cent in this study, which is a higher figure than in, for example, Sweden (57 per cent) and the UK (less than 20 per cent).

Scientists believe that the reason cats from pet shops are more aggressive is because they have not been socialized from a young age. In Sweden it's not permitted to sell or keep cats in pet shops. Neutering usually means that cats become calmer, which has been shown in several studies, even though it's not entirely clear why this is the case.

Are certain types of people more likely to be attacked by an angry cat? In another study from Spain, Jorge Palacio and his colleagues studied who in a family was most vulnerable to cats' attacks. They analysed almost a thousand cases where people had visited health centres in Valencia after being attacked by a cat. The reason why many people visit doctors after being bitten or scratched by a cat is that there is rabies infection in this area. A bite from a rabies-infected cat can transfer this deadly disease to humans. However, none of the cats carried the virus.

The cat attacks weren't triggered by a disease but by conscious provocations from people during play. Women and children usually play more with cats and they were also the most vulnerable to cat attacks. Among children, injuries to hands (32 per cent) and arms (30 per cent) were the most common, followed by head injuries (19 per cent) and leg injuries (17 per cent).

We don't know why some cats become aggressive when their owner just pets them. One theory is that the cat becomes overstimulated but we don't understand the cat's signals; another is that the cat tries to control the situation and decides when it's had enough touching. A third theory is that we pet incorrectly: we often run our hand along the length of the cat's body instead of concentrating on a smaller area in the way cats do when they groom each other.

Another reason cats become aggressive towards humans is unrelated to either play or petting, but fear. You might be close to the cat when something unpleasant happens that the cat can't control, for example a sudden loud noise, a dog coming too close, or two cats fighting outside the window. The fear can then manifest itself in the form of aggression towards you or another cat in the household that it's usually good friends with. And the cat then associates this fear with you or its cat friend long after the frightening moment has passed. Finally, some cats can be unusually aggressive in a way that is best described as a display of social dominance over humans, perhaps when guests are visiting. Such a cat regards the human as any other cat.

To get to grips with aggressive behaviour, it's best to work pre-emptively. Sometimes it's more of a challenge if the cat carries less sociable genes, or if it wasn't socialized enough as a kitten (see the section on secure upbringing earlier in this chapter). The veterinarians Melissa Bain and Elizabeth Stelow from California compiled a checklist with useful measures the owner can take to decrease the amount of aggressive behaviour towards humans (see the table below).

Cats are much more likely to be aggressive towards other cats than towards humans. When cats are aggressive to each other, it's related to finding their place within the group. A cat that has been alone in a household for several years can have a big

Measures to decrease a cat's aggression towards humans

Maintenance	Enrich the home with hiding places, elevated resting places, multiple food stations and litter trays. Play a lot and often with the cat. Avoid as much as possible conflicts that can trigger aggression. Allow cats the opportunity to be outside.
Habituation/ weaning	Don't punish the cat for unwanted behaviour, but postpone treatment temporarily. Give the cat a treat or food when it's behaving well. Approach the cat slowly as long as it's not showing fear or aggression. Wait for the cat to approach you at its own pace. If the cat becomes aggressive when you pet it, slowly increase the time you spend handling and playing with the cat.
Physical health	Rule out or treat underlying medical problems. Neuter the cat.
Mental health	Use a pheromone spray or diffuser to calm your cat. Serotonin-enhancing antidepressant medication can be given to cats.

problem accepting another cat (see 'How many cats should I have?' in Chapter 1). The guiding principles are to introduce the cats to each other gradually and to praise good behaviour.

Don't forget, however, that cats – especially kittens – wrestle and chase each other during play. The intensity of the play will then determine if it's a problem or not. If a real fight breaks out, the cats usually separate into different corners to calm down. That's normal behaviour. But it's not normal if one of the cats show signs of surrender – for example, by lying on its back with its paws stretched upwards – and the other cat keeps attacking. Then it's time to temporarily separate the cats.

SCIENTISTS EXPLAIN

Aggressive cats

- Cat owners often ask vets for advice on how to get to grips with their cats' aggressive behaviour.
- Aggression is one of the most common causes of cats being left at rehoming centres.
- The most common situations when the cats display aggression are when humans are petting or playing with them. Another common reason why cats become aggressive towards humans is fear.
- Cats who don't receive enough stimuli may become more aggressive. Cats living alone in the household and only indoors risk becoming understimulated.

- Socialization during a kitten's first weeks is critical for enabling an adult cat to handle challenges without becoming aggressive.
- Neutering usually means that cats become less aggressive.
- Work pre-emptively to avoid aggression in cats.
- If problems have arisen, gradually reintroduce whatever triggers the cat's attacks. Reward often and don't punish.

At the rehoming centre

As more households in the Western world acquire cats, the number of cats left at rehoming centres increases, too. These cats have a variety of backgrounds. Some have kept children company during the summer holidays and then been left behind when the family returned home. Others are abandoned before a holiday because their owner can't find anyone to look after them or they can't afford a cattery. Many are left at rehoming centres because someone in the family has developed an allergy to cats. A large number of cats are taken there because of behavioural problems; they may be over-aggressive towards other pets or urinate indoors. But, regardless of the reason, many volunteer organizations all around the world do an invaluable job in their efforts to find new owners for these cats.

We don't know exactly how many cats are left in rehoming centres. In the USA, it's estimated that it's 'millions' of cats annually. There are almost three million cats in the Netherlands, and just one rehoming organization (the Dutch Society for the Protection of Animals) receives about 35,000 cats annually. In the UK, the Cats Protection charity rehomed 44,000 cats in 2018. Per Eriksson and his colleagues found in an investigation from 2006 that there were 62 cat centres in Sweden which received an estimated 7,400 cats annually. The same year, the Central Bureau of Statistics estimated that there were 1,256,000 cats in Sweden. This means that roughly between 0.6 and 1.5 per cent of Swedish cats are left at rehoming centres every year.

How do cats feel during their time in a rehoming centre? Are they less stressed if they are kept on their own, in pairs or in groups in an enclosure or room? Does it matter if the cats have lived in multi-cat households or been lone cats? Do the cats' gender and age have an influence on how they cope? And how many square metres does each cat need? Are there toys or activities that decrease the cats' stress?

The answers to these questions are interesting in themselves to understand cat behaviour, but they're also relevant for how we should be designing rehoming centres to be the best they can be. Researchers have investigated cats' stress levels in two different ways: by measuring the amount of the stress hormone cortisol in the urine; and through behavioural studies according to the CSS (Cat Stress Score) protocol, which is especially created to measure cats' stress in a rehoming centre. The cat's behaviours are studied and ranked from 1 to 7, where 1 means relaxed and 7 terrified.

An American research team led by Heidi Broadley investigated whether cats that had lived alone were more stressed in rehoming centres than cats that had lived in a multi-cat household. They didn't find any difference. However, all the cats were very stressed for the first few days after their arrival at the centre. This behavioural study confirms results from other studies measuring the amount of cortisol in the urine; the cats were very nervous and agitated for the first three days, but most of them calmed down to a normal stress level. However, it could take a cat several weeks to finally accept staying at the rehoming centre, or even months in some cases.

Understandably, kittens who are often playful and charming are the ones to be adopted first. The longer a cat stays at a rehoming centre the greater is the risk that it will never be adopted. In a study of a rehoming centre in Portugal, Kelly Gouveia and her colleagues found that cats that had lived in the centre for more than seven years were less active and ate less and were more often involved in fights than cats who'd been there for a shorter time. The chances of a troublemaker being adopted when potential owners come to visit is next to zero. Many of these rejected cats are also more prone to various diseases. This is why early adoption is vital for the cat's wellbeing.

According to Mikel Delgado and his colleagues, a cat's personality is more important than its appearance for its chances of adoption. Despite this, an American investigation showed that white cats were three times more likely to be adopted than black cats, and that grey cats were adopted twice as often as black cats. About 13 per cent of the Americans in the study were superstitious, believing that black cats bring bad luck when they cross the road if you don't spit three times over your shoulder. It's clear that the superstition surrounding black cats brings the cats themselves – rather than the humans – bad luck. Interestingly enough, Elizabeth Stelow and her colleagues showed in 2015 that solid-coloured black female cats have a better personality – that is, they are calmer and less aggressive – than female tortoiseshell, black-and-white or grey-and-white cats. So far, the researchers can't explain why this is the case. But if personality is decisive, black cats should be adopted more – not less – often than other cats.

In most rehoming centres the cats live in groups in different rooms. A typical group size in a study of Swedish rehoming centres, for example, was three to five cats. But does group size influence the cats' wellbeing? Swedish law stipulates that groups of cats in a centre must have at least 2 square metres each to move around in. Until 2013, the requirement was only 1 square metre per cat.

Jenny Loberg and Frida Lundmark at the Swedish University of Agricultural Sciences recently studied behaviour when the cats had access to areas of various sizes. The researchers compared the number of aggressive and friendly behaviours in six different groups with 14–15 adult cats in spaces where they had 1, 2 or 4 square metres each to move around in. The results were clear: the size of the space didn't matter, at least not compared to the significance of placing the 'right' cats together in a room. Which cats suit each other seems to be difficult to give any general advice about. The ability to cope with a stay at a rehoming centre doesn't seem to vary between genders, at least not as long as the cats are neutered.

Because cats in rehoming centres seldom or never go outside, it's important that they have access to many different toys and activities to provide an outlet for their energy, and to decrease stress levels. Too high a stress level for a prolonged period increases the risk of infectious diseases, which then can spread like wildfire in a centre. That's why we shouldn't underestimate the significance of toys, especially during a cat's first weeks at a centre when it is at its most stressed.

Dutch scientists at the University of Utrecht found advice that will delight all rehoming centres working on a limited budget: a simple cardboard box for a new arrival is enough to lower its stress levels significantly. The researchers concluded this after ten cats were each given access to a box measuring 39 × 30 × 26 cm, with entrances on both sides. The cats' behaviour was evaluated against the Cat Stress Score and compared to a control group of ten other cats that didn't get a cardboard box.

The cats that had access to a box were less stressed after just one day, and this effect remained until day 14 when there was no longer any difference between the groups. In earlier studies, it's been observed that cats who didn't receive a cardboard box tried to turn their litter tray upside down just to have somewhere to hide.

No one knows exactly why cats love cardboard boxes. Maybe they can escape their problems and hide inside the box to avoid confronting reality. Or maybe they want to lie in wait for potential prey that might to pass by. Smaller spaces like boxes also become

warmer faster than large rooms. Human habitats are in general a little too cold for cats. Humans are the most comfortable in a temperature of 20 degrees; at this thermal neutral zone, we don't use energy to keep us warm or cool us down. The cat's thermal neutral zone is much higher, at 30–36 degrees. A blanket or a towel inside the box can make it feel much warmer and safer for the cat.

 ## SCIENTISTS EXPLAIN

At the rehoming centre

- More and more cats are left at rehoming centres. In the UK it's at least 50,000 cats per year, in the Netherlands 35,000, and in the USA millions.
- All cats, regardless of background and gender, are very stressed during their first days at the centre.
- An empty cardboard box, preferably with a towel or a blanket, makes it easier for a cat to become accustomed to its new environment. The box makes the cat feel safer and enables it to keep itself warm more easily.
- Early adoption is critical for a cat's long-term wellbeing.

At the vet's

When doctors and nurses go on their rounds, the first question they will ask the patients is: 'And how are we feeling today?' Unfortunately, a vet's patients can't give a useful response to this question, so how, then, can we determine how much pain a cat feels after an operation or a treatment?

In a study led by Juliana Brondani from Brazil, a group of cats received placebos, or sugar pills, and three other groups received pain relief from various medications after surgery. The vets then described the cats' reactions when the surgery wound and the abdomen were manually examined. They also compared the cats' behaviour before and after the surgery. A previously active cat which became reclusive and didn't want to move was a clear example of a cat in pain. Lastly, the vets took the cats' blood pressure and pulse. With the exception of pulse, all these tests gave a good indication of whether the cats' pain level corresponded to the amount of pain relief they'd received.

Even if this book has consistently tried to find common traits in cats' behaviour, it's striking what individuals they are. Cats have widely different personality types, which should also influence how stressed they become when visiting the vet. Stress in turn can influence perceived pain and also how long rehabilitation will take. From a specially made protocol, the South African vet Gareth Zeiler described the temperament of 35 cats that were due for neutering in an animal hospital. He found five different personality types: friendly and extrovert, friendly and shy, reclusive and averse, reclusive and aggressive and, finally, openly aggressive.

For a cat in the latter group it's more or less impossible to assess its pain. Only for the first-named group, the friendly and extroverted cats, is it possible for a vet conclusively to assess the degree of pain a cat experiences. For the other groups there's a risk that the cats are hiding their real pain. Gareth Zeiler discovered that most cats became less stressed at the animal hospital three days after being admitted. Interestingly enough, this result mirrors how cats who are left at rehoming centres react (see the section on rehoming centres above). Cats seem to accept their new situation after three to four days, regardless of whether it's a rehoming centre or an animal hospital.

The cat's personality type and temperament can also affect its risk of becoming ill. Cats can be described as proactive when they quickly take advantage of a new situation, often through aggressive moves towards other cats. Reactive cats, however, are careful when they're put in a new situation and passively await the reaction of the other cats.

Eugenia Natoli and her colleagues showed in feral cats in Rome that proactive males were fathers to more young. But because these males were involved in more fights, they were also more often afflicted with feline AIDS. They had to pay a high price for their breeding success. Luckily, the virus doesn't spread from parents to their offspring.

Male cats are at more risk of being in traffic accidents than females. In an English study, the risk of males being run over is almost twice as high as for females. Males have larger home areas and probably cross more roads, or it's their personality type that exposes them to more risks than females. But the older the cats become the more street smart they are; the risk of a traffic accident decreases by 16 per cent for every year of life. After surviving a traffic accident, many cats become more nervous and usually avoid roads.

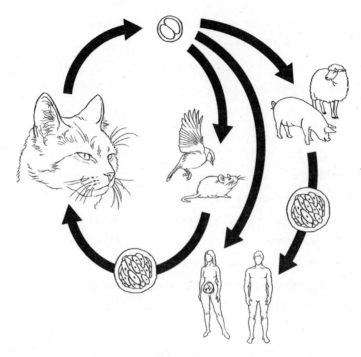

The cat is the main host for the parasite Toxoplasma gondii. *A newly infected cat excretes the parasite's eggs in its faeces. Voles, mice, rats and birds can ingest these eggs and become intermediate hosts for the parasite. A cat becomes infected when it eats an infected intermediate host. Humans can acquire the parasite when they eat lamb or pork that hasn't been properly cooked. More uncommonly, humans can pick up the eggs when they empty a litter tray.*

A disease that's been noticed in the past few years is toxoplasmosis, caused by the one-celled parasite *Toxoplasma gondii*. This parasite can be transmitted from cat to human and is – together with rabies, psittacosis and epidemic nephropathy – an example of zoonosis, a disease that can be transmitted from animals to humans. The cat is the main host for the parasite, but seldom shows symptoms.

A large proportion of healthy cats have antibodies against the parasite, which shows they've been infected but are now immune. In the area around Uppsala, Sweden, vets found antibodies against the parasite in 42 per cent of all examined cats. Cats are usually infected when they eat diseased rodents or birds, and can in turn transmit the disease to humans through their faeces.

It should be underlined, however, that there is no conclusive connection between cat ownership and toxoplasmosis in humans. The most common way for humans to be infected is to ingest the parasite by eating meat from lamb or pork that hasn't been heated to a safe temperature. Most people infected by the parasite don't notice any symptoms, but toxoplasmosis can be dangerous to foetuses, so women should avoid emptying litter trays during pregnancy.

In a recently published study in the journal *Brain, Behavior and Immunity* it was estimated that around 30 per cent of all humans in the word are infected by toxoplasmosis without any visible symptoms. But a dangerous effect of having cysts filled with toxoplasma parasites in the brain has been found lately. The disease makes rats less afraid of cats, and they are even drawn to the smell of cat urine. In other words, the parasite affects the behaviour of the intermediate host rat so it is more easily predated by the cat. From there, the parasite is spread to the main host, the cat, where it can reproduce.

In humans, toxoplasmosis is now being suspected as a factor behind personality changes like aggression, depression and increased risk of suicide. Scientists have also found a connection between toxoplasmosis and a reduced ability to react and concentrate. This could explain why infected individuals are at a higher risk of being involved in traffic accidents.

SCIENTISTS EXPLAIN

At the vet's

- A cat's perception of pain can be measured by taking its blood pressure and studying its behaviour.
- Very stressed cats probably conceal their pain.
- After about three days, cats in animal hospitals become less stressed.
- Males are more often involved than females in traffic accidents and more likely to be afflicted by diseases such as feline AIDS.
- The cat is the main host for the one-celled parasite *Toxoplasma gondii*, and a large proportion of all cats have been or are carriers of the parasite. The disease toxoplasmosis can be transmitted to humans through a cat's faeces.
- In most cases, toxoplasmosis is harmless except for the unborn child, so pregnant women should avoid emptying the litter tray.

5

The cat and the human

WHEN A PET cat comes into your home, your life will change for ever. Researchers have shown that children who grow up with a pet have better body language and self-esteem. New cat owners have improved physical and mental health. The cat's health, in turn, is influenced by our lifestyle. We have increasingly less time for play and exercise, while the cats receive better veterinary care and food. This chapter discusses the interaction between the cat and the human, as well as the interaction between the cat and the dog.

Like cats and dogs

Everyone has probably heard the expression 'to fight like cats and dogs', meaning to always argue or disagree. Cats and dogs that don't know each other probably do disagree. But what's it like for cats and dogs that are forced to live under the same roof? Can they learn to tolerate, or even appreciate, each other?

In North America and many countries in Europe, the cat is now a more common pet than the dog. In Europe in 2012 there were 90 million domestic cats and 75 million dogs, according to the European Pet Food Industry Federation. And cats and dogs are increasingly living under the same roof. Many people probably still feel hesitant about having both as pets because of that enduring expression, 'to fight like cats and dogs'.

The dog originates from the wolf *Canis lupus,* and, according to archaeological findings, the wolf was domesticated 14,000 years ago. Genetic studies now show that it could have happened long before that, maybe even as far back as 100,000 years ago. The domestic cat originates from the African wildcat *Felis silvestris lybica.* Many believe that the Egyptians first domesticated the wildcat about 4,000 years ago, but recent archaeological findings on Cyprus suggest that the cat was domesticated 9,500 years ago (see Chapter 1).

The cat's main role initially was to keep vermin like rats, mice and birds away from grain stores. In exchange, they received shelter and food. Unlike dogs – and also other domesticated animals like cows, horses, sheep and pigs – there hasn't been a deliberate selection of desired behaviours in cats. So the cat is both physiologically and behaviourally less domesticated, or wilder if you will, than the dog.

Both cats and dogs belong to an order of predators (Carnivora) whose members are skilful and aggressive hunters. But their behaviours differ: the dog lives and hunts in packs while the cat is a lone hunter and is seen as antisocial. Both species communicate through sight, smell, hearing and physical contact, and they display a great ability to learn by observation. Both dog and cat use body language to show things like dominance, aggression and fear. But the same behaviour can have a very different meaning in a dog and a cat.

Two scientists from Israel recently looked more closely at the interaction between cats and dogs living in the same household. They used two research methods to find out more. First, they interviewed the owners, and then they made systematic observations of how their cats and dogs interacted. For the study they used only animals over six months old because younger animals haven't yet established stable behaviour patterns. They also omitted households where the animals lived mostly outside.

A total of 154 households answered 28 questions about their pets' backgrounds (age, gender and so on) and how they interacted. From these households, 45 were chosen for careful, systematic observations of the pets' behaviour. The cat and the dog were first fed and then they were shut together in a room familiar to them for three hours. Two observers and their owner were also in the room, and all behaviours and interactions were recorded on video.

Three tests lasting 20 minutes were conducted. The first was a play test, where a tennis ball was rolled between the dog and the cat to see whether they played together or showed any dominant or submissive behaviour. Then there was an owner test, where the owner placed a bowl of wet food between the animals. Lastly, the owner encouraged play between dog and cat. All behaviours were categorized into one of five different classes: dominance; fear/submission; aggression; play; and attempted closeness. The researchers were looking particularly for behaviours that differed between dog and cat (see table below).

The meaning of body language in dogs and cats

BODY LANGUAGE	MEANING IN CATS	MEANING IN DOGS
Stretching Out Front Legs	Aggressive	Friendly, submissive
Lying On Back	Aggressive	Submissive
Turning Head Away	Aggressive, dominating	Submissive
Moving The Tail	Aggressive (the whole tail), playful, hunting (tip of tail only)	Friendly, submissive

The answers from the owners showed that in less than a tenth of households the relationship between dog and cat was seen as aggressive, and in a quarter of the households the dog and the cat were indifferent to each other. But in most cases they were reasonably friendly. In the various tests, it transpired that the cat displayed more aggression, playfulness and fear/submissiveness than the dog. Half of the dog's behaviours were attempts at approaching the cat while the cat wasn't at all interested in coming closer to the dog.

A play test was one of the ways the scientists studied the interaction between a dog and cat from the same household.

In the next stage, the researchers studied the significance of the pets' backgrounds on their behaviour. They investigated, among other things, the significance of gender, whether they'd been neutered, whether the dog or the cat was the first to be introduced into the household, and at the age they were at the time. They found that female cats displayed more aggression towards dogs than male cats. When the cat was the pet before the dog, they became friends more easily than vice versa. And it worked particularly well if the cat was less than six months old and the dog less than a year old when they met for the first time. They could read each other's body language better then, especially those behaviours that have different meanings in a dog and a cat.

It's clear that a dog and a cat can get on well together despite the big differences in body language and their different levels of domestication. If you are hesitating about getting a cat when you already have a dog, or vice versa, you can feel reassured. Dogs are well known for being able to initiate play more often with animals other than their own species. Many dogs in households with a cat will also learn to greet the cat nose to nose as cats do, and not nose to bottom as two dogs do.

It's perhaps not surprising that a sociable animal like the dog turns out to be so adaptable. However, the researchers were surprised that the dog had difficulties adapting to a new cat if the dog was the first in the household. Dogs were friendlier towards cats when they came last into the household and more aggressive when they were first. A reasonable interpretation of this result is that dogs are mentally and emotionally more dependent on their owner than cats. A dog that was the first pet in the household will be more 'jealous' of a new cat when the attention it's used to decreases in relation to the cat's arrival. Both dog and cat have a critical period when very young (from two to nine weeks) when their social behaviours are formed, so it's not particularly surprising that they will have a better chance of getting on well if they're introduced to each other at a young age.

Felines and canines obviously have a common past, long before humans domesticated them. An international research team led by Daniele Silvestro from Gothenburg University showed recently that felines were usually more efficient predators than canines, which contributed to several dog species becoming extinct. The dog family has its origins in North America about 40 million years ago; 22 million years ago there were more than 30 dog species on that continent. The cat family has its origins in Asia but once felines eventually arrived in North America, they contributed to the extinction of most canines. Today there are only nine species of the dog family left in North America. Competition for the limited amount of prey allowed only the largest canines to survive.

SCIENTISTS EXPLAIN

Like cats and dogs

- A dog and a cat living under the same roof can often enjoy each other's company and improve each other's quality of life.
- A dog and a cat can even learn to understand each other's body language, despite the fact that certain types of behaviour mean very different things in dog and cat.
- A dog and a cat will get on better if their first meeting happens when they are very young (the cat less than six months old, the dog less than a year old).
- It's better to introduce a cat into a household first. A dog will have a harder time adapting to the shared attention if it arrives before a cat.

The cat's effect on our health

Do you know why you acquired a cat? Was it the children's pestering that finally paid off? Or was it a spur-of-the-moment decision when you saw the charming kitten in the litter or re-homing centre? Maybe it was the cat that got you, just as in Nils Uddenberg's wonderful story, *The Old Man and the Cat*, where a stray a cat takes on – and gets into – a new family. Regardless of the reason, you've probably got a winning ticket in life. You are going to feel better, have an better quality of life, and better health. But how can cats have these positive effects on our health?

Growing up with a cats offers a child many advantages for their social development. Andrew Edney showed this in a summary article published in the *Journal of the Royal Society of Medicine*. Children with pets have better body language and self-esteem, as well as better social skills than children who grow up without pets.

Children also see that cats are still loved despite being told off by adults. Cats often become a natural part of small children's play, and they can 'listen' to a child's secrets without telling anyone else. And sad children always get comfort from cats without having to reciprocate. Children with pets encounter life's joys and sorrows – births and deaths, diseases and recoveries – earlier in life than children without pets. They are simply better prepared for life as adults. Andrew Edney has even suggested that the risk of children becoming criminals later in life is reduced if pets are in the family. That might be the case, because it's certainly true that cats can contribute to a child's social development.

When children grow up and become teenagers, they often spend much less time with their pets. In an interview study of almost thousand teenagers in Australia, it turned out that more than 80 per cent of them had a dog or cat in the household. But these teenagers hardly interacted with their pets; only every tenth day and less than 1 per cent of all their waking hours were dedicated to them. It's not surprising, then, that the researchers found no sign that these pets had any influence on the teenagers' physical or mental wellbeing.

These results contradict the results of investigations on adult humans, where pets have repeatedly been shown to have positive effects on our physical and mental health. For example, in an English interview study conducted by James Serpell, 24 new cat owners were asked about their general health and physical wellbeing the day after they got their first cat. Serpell then asked the same questions a month later, six months later and, finally, ten months later. The cat owners thought they had far fewer problems with their general health after a month compared to when they first got their cat. This effect lingered until six months, then disappeared after ten months.

It's difficult to explain why cat owners' perceived health first became better and then fell back to normal. Maybe it was the placebo effect, that is, they expected to feel better and and so felt better? Or perhaps it was the novelty of having the company of a cat for the first time that affected their health positively?

It isn't just perceived health that is influenced by having a cat. During medical tests, doctors have observed decreased blood pressure and lower levels of cholesterol in patients with a pet. Even the chances of surviving after surgery for acute myocardial infarction increased in pet owners. The chances of survival for a year after surgery increased the most if there was a dog in the household, probably because dog owners are more active and go for long walks more than cat owners. This obviously has a positive effect on health. We can become just as attached to a cat as a dog, however, and for many people the cat can work as a substitute for human contact, a friend or even a child.

When we speak to a cat, we often use a type of baby language with high pitch and exaggerated emotions (happiness, interest, surprise, anger and so on). Do we subconsciously try to teach our pets to speak by using baby language? In an article in *Science* journal, Denis Burnham and his colleagues investigated how 12 mothers pronounced the words 'shoe', 'sheep' and 'shark' when they spoke to their six-month-old child, cat or dog, and partner. The mothers used a higher pitch and a wider spectrum of emotions when they spoke to their baby and pet compared to their partner. However, the exaggerated emphasis on vowels was something used exclusively for babies.

Regardless of whether the language is English, Russian, Swedish or Japanese, parents emphasize vowels as a pedagogical trick to stimulate their children's language development. Scientists believe that we adapt our way of speaking to meet the receiver's requirements. That's why we use a higher pitch and strong emotions with our pets, so they will better understand us, but because we don't expect them to start speaking we don't emphasize the vowels as much.

There are two different theories about why cats are so popular with humans: attachment theory and the theory of social support. According to attachment theory the cat can be compared to a child, and the owner has a largely parenting and nurturing role. According to the theory of social support, the relationship is more equal between cat and human, and the cat functions as another member of the owner's social network, which can give emotional support when life is particularly difficult.

Karin Stammbach and Dennis Turner explored these theories through an interview study of 370 women from Switzerland. It wasn't particularly surprising that the results showed support for both theories, depending on the family situation. The more people there were in a household the less time was spent on the cat, which in turn decreased the affection for the cat. But for owners who lived in single-person households, the cat functioned as a family member offering emotional support. If single female owners had a large social network, the need for social support from the cat decreased to a corresponding degree.

Without a doubt, the cat plays a large part in our everyday life. The support we experience from cats makes us look past behavioural problems like clawing furniture or not using the litter tray properly. The cat has an undeserved reputation for being a recluse that doesn't show affection. Most cats greet us when we come home, want to lie in our lap when we read a book or watch television, tell us when it's time to play, and sleep in our bed at night. Their interaction is also the main reason why we like cats. Unlike humans, the cat's affection is unconditional, and despite our mood swings the cat always accepts us just as we are.

You can take advantage of the cat's positive effects even if you don't have a cat waiting for you at home. The American scientist Jessica Myrick interviewed 6,500 people to investigate how their mood was affected by watching cat videos. Many of us will postpone a difficult task to watch a cat video on the Internet instead, and our feelings of guilt come as an inevitable consequence. It turns out, however, that the guilty feelings are counterbalanced by a feeling of elation afterwards. In fact, the people who were interviewed became more efficient at work after their short break.

According to a Japanese research team led by Hiroshi Nittono, concentration and efficiency at work increase the most when the test subjects look at pictures of kittens or puppies. Pictures of cute animals trigger positive emotions, which in turn make us more focused and thorough in our job.

SCIENTISTS EXPLAIN

The cat's effect on our health

- Children who grow up with cats have better body language and self-esteem, as well as superior social skills, than children who grow up without a pet.
- Adults who get a cat perceive their health improving significantly, at least during the first six months.
- Medical tests show that pet owners have reduced blood pressure and cholesterol levels.
- Cats offer us affection and social support. Depending on our family situation and the extent of our social network, cats can be seen as a member of the family.
- The main reason we like cats is because they interact with us: they greet us when we come home, enjoy playing with us and sleep next to us.

The cat's health and wellbeing

Cat owners are generally good at interpreting their cats' behaviour and body language. We understand when they want to go outside, eat or play, but how do we know what we need to do for them to have good health and wellbeing in the long term? Humans have a tendency to project their own thoughts and motives on to cats, which can lead to incorrect conclusions. Anthropomorphism – giving animals human characteristics – is a problem when we try to assess a pet's quality of life.

Many cat owners will say that their cat has complex emotions; they can feel guilty after having done something bad or proud when they've done something good. But even with our closest relative, the chimpanzee, science has had difficulty proving such emotions. For example, your cat is not punishing you by urinating in your open suitcase when you've been away. Cats can't have such complicated thought processes. However, it probably feels uncomfortable with the suitcase's new smells and wants to 'neutralize' them. A punishment in this case can lead to worse behavioural problems. We should be careful about castigating 'guilty' pets, because they don't understand why we are doing it.

In an English investigation, 76 per cent of owners perceived their cat as a family member. And the same proportion thought their cat was the perfect one. That we want the best for our cats goes

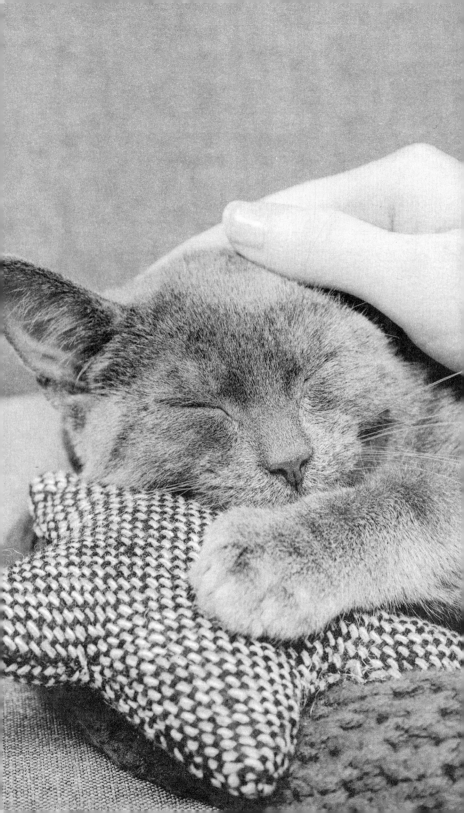

without saying. In 2005, in the journal *Applied Animal Behaviour Science*, Irene Rochlitz presented a list of the cat's most basic requirements for it to have good health and wellbeing (see the table below). This list can obviously be expanded and refined, but if the basic requirements aren't met, the cat won't have a pleasant life.

The cat's five basic requirements

1	**Access to food and water**	A balanced diet which meets the cat's nutritional requirements at all stages of life; continual access to fresh water.
2	**An appropriate living environment**	Enough space and protection from weather and wind, enough light, low noise levels, clean space, either just indoors or with freedom to go outside.
3	**Access to health and medical care**	Vaccination, neutering, control of both internal (e.g. worms) and external (e.g. ticks) parasites, ID chipping, quick access to veterinary care when needed.
4	**Natural behaviour**	Opportunities to have an outlet for all natural behaviour towards other cats as well as humans.
5	**Freedom from fear**	Protection from situations that could lead to fear and anxiety.

Across the world, increased urbanization – human migration from the countryside to cities – affects our pet cats' wellbeing. Humans increasingly live in smaller spaces and work longer days. We're often forced to move to new places or travel regularly for work. Pets are expected to be adaptable despite us having less time for them. A consequence of urbanization is that we have more pets in a smaller space or fewer pets per household. Both of these situations can affect a cat's wellbeing negatively: in multi-cat households in cramped spaces, the cats can't escape each other, which leads to an increased chance of conflict, and single cats often don't get enough social interaction. A third of all cats living in cities today therefore have some kind of behavioural disorder.

In Sweden, for example, the number of cats in Stockholm county has decreased dramatically in the past few years, from 104 cats per thousand inhabitants in 2006 to 65 cats per thousand inhabitants in 2012. And this while cats have increased in many other counties during the same time. A reasonable explanation is that we care about the cat's health and wellbeing and avoid getting a cat when we live in large cities and smaller spaces. Very few cats living in city centres are allowed outdoors and consequently they don't have an outlet for their natural behaviour. But it's important to remember that – just as there are risks in just letting a cat stay indoors – there are great risks for the cat's health and wellbeing out of doors as well (see the table below).

Risks to health and wellbeing for indoor and outdoor cats

RISKS FOR A CAT LIVING EXCLUSIVELY INDOORS	RISKS FOR A CAT ALLOWED OUTDOORS
Feline lower urinary tract disease	Infectious diseases (viruses, parasites)
Feline tooth resorption (TR)	Traffic accidents
Hyperthyroidism (overactive thyroid)	Other accidents (for example falls from trees)
Becoming overweight	Fights with other cats
Household dangers (for example accidents, poisoning)	Attacks from dogs or other animals
Inactivity	Poisoning
Behavioural problems (for example not using the litter tray)	Theft
Boredom	Running away

In her overview article in *Journal of Veterinary Behavior,* Ellen Jongman showed that indoor cats need access to at least two rooms, and if there is more than one cat in the household the rooms should be large enough for them to be able to be at least 3 metres from each other. The quality of the space, however, is more important than the amount of living space itself.

There should be vertical structures for them to climb, an opportunity to survey their surroundings from an elevated spot like a hat rack or bookshelf, several different resting and sleeping places, places to hide and opportunities to sit by a window and look out, a scratching post or cat tree, a litter tray, food and clean water, access to toys that encourage natural behaviours and, lastly, an owner who cuddles and plays with the cat. In multi-cat households, all cats should be neutered and the above environmental factors should apply to each individual cat.

Cats are popular because they easily adapt to life with humans. Giuseppe Piccione and his colleagues wanted to investigate whether they even adjust something as basic as their circadian rhythm to their owners'. In their experiment a group of five cats moved freely during the day between a large house and an enclosed garden, but at night they were kept outside. Another group of five cats were in a smaller house and let outside into a smaller yard for only an hour in the morning. It transpired that the cats left outside all night maintained their natural circadian rhythm: they slept during the day and were active all night. The other group lived almost in symbiosis with the human, and adjusted their circadian rhythm to the human's. Their peak of activity was noticed in the morning – just before their owner went to work – and again in the evening when the owner returned home.

Is your cat often waiting for you by the door when you come home at night? Could your cat be sleeping all day and waking up just in time for you to come home? In other words, is your cat psychic? The theory about pets' supernatural powers received a lot of space in the 1990s after Rupert Sheldrake published his book *Seven Experiments That Could Change the World*. To try to find answers to this question, the researchers Richard Wiseman and Matthew Smith arranged several experiments that all showed that the animals weren't clairvoyant. The most likely explanation is that your pet goes back and forth to the door several times a day, but you only notice when it coincides with your arrival home. So it's much more plausible that this is your cat's standard routine rather than supernatural powers.

The perfect living room for cats, where they can rest, survey their domain, hide, scratch, play and relax with their owner.

The cat's health and wellbeing is largely influenced by access to a good living environment, with everything that entails. But social factors are also important. Cats that have been socialized at a young age are often affectionate. And the emotional bond between you and your cat is strengthened if you speak, pet and play with the cat. But the outcome of these interactions also depends on both your personalities and how well they interact.

Manuela Wedl and her colleagues from Austria investigated whether humans' and cats' ways of interacting differed according to their gender. It turned out that the cat's gender didn't matter at all. However, female owners had a closer relationship to their cats than men. Women spoke to their cats more often and spent more time with them. The women spent one to two hours a day with the cat while she gave it food, emptied the litter tray, played with it and cuddled it. Maybe it's not so strange, then, that cats seek contact with women more often than men?

Wedl's investigation also showed that the owner's personality mattered. A neurotic owner sought contact with their cat more often, which in turn made the cat want less contact. The cat always had an advantage and there was an imbalance in the relationship. If the cat sought contact first, the interaction lasted longer than if the owner initiated contact because the cat often lost interest more quickly.

Owners who didn't display big mood swings from one day to the next, but instead showed reliable behaviour, had a more balanced relationship with the cat. An owner who in most cases accepts the cat's invitations to interact gets the cat's attention in return when the owner is in a playful mood. But if the owner turns down the cat's invitations too often, there could be a downward spiral. It's a bargaining game.

But more play isn't always better in the cat's world. Of course, your cat will become calmer and have fewer problems if you give it more attention and interact with it during the day. But the cat doesn't always want to play, and too much forced play can make a cat insecure in the long run. Some argue that the cat's desire to socialize with humans only comes from it wanting food. But that is definitely not the motive every time, according to Manuela Wedl. Cats also seek contact with 'their' humans, because they're raised to be social creatures that need play and closeness.

We give our cats ever better veterinary care and improved and higher-quality food, but at the same time we have less time for play and exercise. Vets in the USA see more cases of obesity, anxiety and obsessive compulsive disorders in cats as a consequence of this changing lifestyle. The German scientists Ellen Kienzle and Reinhold Bergler were interested in the phenomenon of overweight cats. They interviewed 60 owners of overweight cats – males over 6 kilograms and females over 5 kilograms – as well as 60 owners of cats of normal weight. It turned out that owners of overweight cats weren't particularly happy before they got their cat, and the reason they got it was to gain comfort and support. The cat became a replacement for human interactions.

Most owners of overweight cats often watched them when they were eating, while owners of normal-weight cats didn't as often. The researchers believe that the owners of overweight cats used the food as a reward and as a way of communicating with the cat. These cats also received treats or food directly from the human's plate more often. A reward for cats of normal weight was usually not food but more time for play. The researchers could find no differences between the cat owners in the two groups in terms of weight, age, family status, education or income.

Finally, the effect of breeding on the health and wellbeing of pure-bred cats should be mentioned. The breeding of cats isn't as prevalent as it is for dogs. In Sweden, 9 per cent of all cats are pure bred according to Statistics Sweden, while 75 to 80 per cent of all dogs are pure bred according to the Swedish Kennel Club. Pure-bred cats are assessed from established criteria for how they should look, and this appearance doesn't always go hand in hand with the cat's wellbeing. For example, when Persians have difficulties eating you could question whether their wellbeing has been prioritized. Because the number of breeding males is limited in many cat breeds, they gradually lose their genetic diversity, which increases the risk of harmful genes being expressed.

SCIENTISTS EXPLAIN

The cat's health and wellbeing

- For a cat to have a good quality of life, it's vital that its basic needs are met (for food, water, a good living environment, healthcare, an outlet for natural behaviours, and a chance to avoid fear and anxiety).
- More cats are at risk of having behavioural disorders as a consequence of increased urbanization.
- Most cats have an outlet for their natural behaviours out-doors, but many dangers also lurk outside.
- Cats that live only indoors adjust their circadian rhythm to the humans'.
- Women spend more time with cats than men, and cats seek contact more often with women than men.
- If humans force themselves on a cat too often, it will lead to the cat withdrawing.
- Cats that are acquired as a replacement for human interaction have a higher risk of becoming overweight.
- Fewer than 10 per cent of all cats in Sweden are pure bred. In some breeds there is a risk that the desired appearance does not always go hand in hand with good health.

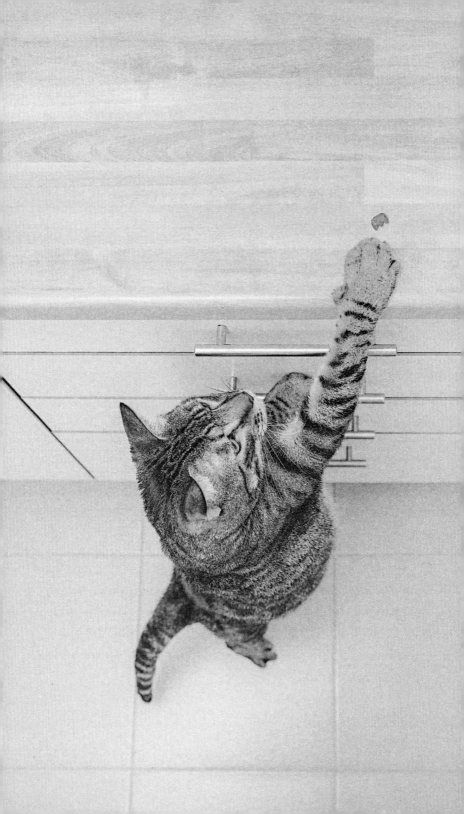

6

The cat at home

THE INDUSTRY AROUND the production of cat food, litter trays, litter, pet beds and toys for cats turns over more than £8 billion per year in Europe and the USA. But is there scientific support for a certain type of food, litter or toy that is better than another? In this chapter, you will learn that more expensive isn't necessarily better.

Food preferences

We've all seen the cat food commercials, with slogans like 'Cats know the difference' and 'Eight out of ten cats prefer it'. Cat owners in ads often talk of the advantages of a particular make of cat food: 'It both looks and smells better than other cat food'; 'I know how important basic ingredients are for the flavour, and my cat knows that too.'

Sometimes it's said that cat food producers have a customer with six legs: one with four legs that eats the food and one with two legs who chooses it. But is there scientific evidence for the pouches' and tins' enticing slogans like 'science diet', 'prescription diet', 'veterinary formulated' or 'proactive'? What does the research say about what your cat actually needs?

The cat food industry has shown steady growth, and there is no lack of scientific articles on what type of food domestic cats prefer. So much has been written in recent years that several overview articles have been published. The most comprehensive of these was published in 1984 in the journal *Annual Review of Nutrition*, where M. L. MacDonald and colleagues summarized the results of more than 250 articles. In this compilation of knowledge, we are reminded that the cat is predominantly a predator that demands only meat on the menu.

Unlike the dog, which is also a predator (belonging to the order Carnivora), the cat doesn't need carbohydrates like rice and vegetables. It's a strict carnivore that needs first and foremost good-quality proteins, preferably from muscles and not connective tissue. This is especially important for kittens, which need almost twice as much protein by weight as adult cats (17 as against 10 per cent).

Wildcats – which catch living prey – ingest no carbohydrates at all. While domestic cats don't need food with added carbohydrates in the form of rice, peas or grains, several studies have shown that adult cats can break down and absorb most carbohydrates. But because the activity of enzymes which can break down sugar in the liver is very low – compared to an omnivore like the dog – cats avoid eating sugary food. By contrast, the amino acid taurine is essential for cats. It's mainly needed for sight, heart health and reproduction, and cats can't overdose on taurine in food.

Cats like and need a certain amount of fat in their food. In an experiment, cats preferred food that contained 25 per cent fat to food with 10 or 50 per cent fat. Maybe this result depends more on the food's consistency than its taste: if its fat content is too low the food becomes dry, and if it's too high it becomes too oily. Cats who are active and spend time outdoors often may need food with a high fat content. A neutered indoor cat, however, has a lower metabolism and shouldn't eat food containing more than about 10 per cent fat.

A wildcat uses more energy than a domestic cat, and needs to eat 360 calories per day, or the equivalent of eight to 12 mice. Since the wildcat has to work hard to catch prey, it will tend to focus on capturing larger prey. Wildcats don't eat carcasses, preferring fresh meat. They're opportunists and can leave their dinner if an opportunity arises to catch new prey. Domestic cats, on the other hand, often have free access to dry food all day and will eat little and often, frequently 12 to 20 times over 24 hours; it doesn't eat more often during the daytime.

A domestic cat that can eat whenever it wants and doesn't get enough exercise risks becoming fat. Just like humans across large parts of the Western world, the number of cats becoming overweight or obese has increased dramatically since the 1970s. In the UK and the USA today it's estimated that at least one in three cats is overweight. Because fat cats have an increased risk of developing diabetes and problems with their joints, heart and lungs, scientists are paying a lot of attention to possible weight reduction methods.

One of these experiments was conducted by Jon Ramsey and his colleagues and the results were published in the *American Journal of Veterinary Research*. They wanted to find out whether it was possible for cats to lose weight by giving them wet food instead of dry. Five cats received wet food from a known brand for three weeks, while five other cats got exactly the same food but the researchers had freeze-dried the content (removed the water).

After a three-week pause during which all the cats received dry food, they repeated the experiment, but the cats who had received wet food in the first experiment now had freeze-dried food, and vice versa. The researchers replaced the food twice a day so that all the cats had access to fresh food the whole time.

Although the study lasted only a short while, the effect was clear: a diet of only wet food made the cats lose weight. The cats also preferred to eat the wet food instead of the freeze-dried version of the wet food. But because dry food is good for reducing tooth loss – a common problem among older cats – dry food of good quality but low in calories may be preferable to a diet of only wet food for overweight cats.

Anyone who has a cat knows that they can be fastidious about their food. Their food should be at room temperature; if it's too hot or too cold, the cat will ignore it until it's reached the optimal temperature. Very small differences in the food's smell, flavour, texture and composition can also lead to the cat rejecting food that it would otherwise readily eat, at least if the cat is used to being given an alternative if the first food offered is rejected. But it may be a good thing to be choosy: it turns out that cats quickly learn to avoid poisonous food and food lacking vital amino acids or vitamins. Many cats are also suspicious of new dishes on the menu. Just like small children, they sometimes display neophobia, a fear of new things – in this case foods. 'You know what you have, but not what you can get ...'

Several researchers investigated whether house cats and farm cats have different food preferences. Can individual taste preferences be due to the food they experienced when young? And are house cats more choosy because they've not received as varied a diet as farm cats? In England, John Bradshaw and his colleagues investigated the food preferences of 28 house cats and 36 farm cats from three different farms. All the cats got to choose from dry food, wet food based on fish, wet food based on meat, and raw and cooked mince.

The results showed large differences between house cats and farm cats. House cats avoided raw mince while farm cats gobbled it up. They even preferred the raw mince over the cooked. Because the house cats hadn't encountered raw mince earlier in life, this was a typical case of neophobia.

Farm cats are forced to be more opportunistic because they don't get as much food and they eat less often. The farm cats greedily ate the unfamiliar dishes such as the wet food based on meat and fish. However, they avoided the dry food, probably because it was too painful to eat; most farm cats have feline calicivirus (cat flu) and one of the symptoms is mouth ulcers. So the farm cats didn't display the same reluctance to try new foods; in fact, they preferred dishes that they hadn't encountered before to their usual food.

John Bradshaw also investigated the food preferences of feral cats. It was estimated that in 1996 there were 1–2 million feral cats in English urban parks and on wasteland. These cats certainly can't be too choosy when they forage in garbage to supplement their diet, which mostly consists of small birds, voles and mice. Bradshaw's experiments revealed that feral cats preferred unusual food to an even greater extent than farm cats. We don't know yet why this is the case, but the most reasonable explanation is that a varied diet allows feral cats to get more of the nutrients they need. They can't be fastidious but will try most things as long as the smell isn't too repulsive. The spoiled house cat wrinkles its nose at new food while the feral cat happily tries new things. This large range of behaviours shows how well cats can adapt to new situations.

SCIENTISTS EXPLAIN

Food preferences

- The cat is predominantly a predator and prefers to eat fresh meat. Their food should contain protein of high quality and fat. However, the cat normally doesn't eat carbohydrates.
- A house cat will eat 12 to 20 times a day if it has free access to dry food.
- A wildcat needs to consume 360 calories a day, which corresponds to eight to 12 mice.
- At least a third of cats in the UK and the USA are overweight. Wet food works as a slimming diet, but there's a risk that their teeth and gums aren't 'exercised' enough.
- House cats are conservative when it comes to the food they eat. New foods are seldom appreciated. However, they like a variety of food as long as all the food is familiar to them.
- Don't put your cats' food bowl close to the water bowl or the litter tray.
- Farm cats and feral cats will eat most things, probably as way of making sure they get all the vital nutrients, minerals and vitamins they need.
- Most dry food from the shops contains enough proteins and fats. However, tests show that some brands don't have enough of the essential amino acid taurine.
- Dry food can remain in the cat's food bowl for several hours without harm. Wet food is perishable, however, and shouldn't

be out for more than an hour. Keep the opened can of wet food in the fridge.

- Cats shouldn't eat raw fish because it could contain a substance that breaks down vitamin B.

How cats lap

Does a cat really get any water when it laps with its tongue? It doesn't look very efficient. Humans have the advantage of having a fairly small mouth and large cheeks, so that we can create downward pressure that moves the water to our throat. Cats and dogs have big mouths but small cheeks and so they can't create the same downward pressure as humans. And they must usually also fight against gravity when they drink with their head above the water source. Unlike cats, we also don't have to drink with our mouths above the water surface. We can comfortably scoop up the water with our hands or drink from a glass. But what do cats do, then, when they drink?

With modern technology, scientists have now shown how cats drink. What doesn't look especially efficient to the naked eye turns out through the lens of a high-speed camera to be a remarkably elegant and advanced manoeuvre.

In the journal *Science*, Pedro Reis and his colleagues show step by step how it works. With its head above the surface of the water, the cat stretches out the tip of its tongue. And it uses only the smooth tip when it drinks, not the rest of the tongue, which is rough and densely covered with barbs. The tip of the cat's tongue is tilted back when it rests on the water without breaking the water surface. When the cat lifts its tongue, the surface tension creates a pillar of water between the tip of the tongue and the water. Gravitational pull makes this pillar thinner the more the tip is raised above the water surface.

On the Facebook page 'What Does Your Cat Think?' there's a video that shows how it works. The interaction between the surface tension of the water and the gravitational pull determines when the cat laps up the water into its mouth. When the cat has repeated this procedure three to 17 times, there's 10 millilitres of water in its mouth, which the cat then swallows. This is obviously not something the cat is thinking about. It's a technique that's been refined with evolution.

To the naked eye it may seem that the dog laps water in a similar way, but a high-speed camera reveals big differences. The dog's tongue isn't bent down but up, and the tip of the tongue breaks the surface tension. So the tongue creates a bowl which the dog uses when it scoops water into its mouth.

All felines have been shown to use the same technique as the domestic cat, but the bigger the cat the more slowly it laps. So a leopard laps water more slowly than your domestic cat. But the adaptable domestic cat has certain advantages that felines in the wild lack. For example, it can 'trick' gravity. When you let water run from a tap, the cat doesn't have to overcome gravity and can more easily get water into its mouth. It's unclear whether that's the reason many cats prefer to drink water from the tap rather than the bowl. It might be because tap water is fresh or that it's simply more fun for the cat to drink from the tap. Maybe this is another question for a scientist to answer?

Domestic cats that eat mainly canned food, whether it's meat or fish, don't have to drink as much because the food contains much of their water requirement. Cats that usually receive dry food need to drink more. Normally the cat drinks as often as it eats, ten to 15 times a day. Most people who have a cat know that they can be fussy drinkers and are very choosy about the

The tip of the cat's tongue doesn't break the water's surface tension and creates a pillar of water when the cat lifts its tongue.

purity and flavour of the water. All cats, however, have their own peculiarities and you'll have to play it by ear to discover your own cat's drinking preferences.

Drinking fountains are appreciated by many cats. The gurgling water entices the cat to drink more often. If your cat likes to drink from the toilet when you've forgotten to put down the lid, or out of the shower, you can offer an alternative water source by placing a big bowl of water in the bathroom, close to the shower or the toilet.

Do cats get stomach problems if they drink milk or cream instead of water? This is a question vets are often asked, and they always say that we shouldn't give milk to cats. Cats are lactose intolerant: their intestines can't break down the sugars found in milk and dairy products. Even if a cat happily laps a saucer of milk, problems can arise later and the cat won't connect its discomfort to the milk.

 **SCIENTISTS EXPLAIN**

How cats lap

- Cats can't create downward pressure in their mouth like humans, so they have to lap in order to drink.
- The cat lets the bent tip of its tongue rest on the water surface and the tongue doesn't break the surface tension. A water pillar is created when the cat moves its tongue tip into its mouth.
- All felines lap with the same technique but at different speeds.

- Domestic cats that eat only dry food need to drink ten to 15 times a day.
- Don't put food and water bowls close to each other. Cats don't want to risk spoiled food ending up in their drinking water.
- Change your cat's drinking water twice a day and have several different water bowls in the home.
- Avoid plastic bowls as these can taint the water; use bowls made of glass, porcelain or stainless steel instead.
- Don't give cats milk – their stomachs aren't adapted to it.

Which type of cat litter?

It's definitely not easy to find your way through the morass of products sold as cat litter. A quick search on the Internet reveals dozens of brands offering more than a hundred types made from different materials. You can now choose between yellow, blue, green, or pink cat litter. Do you want it to smell like a summer meadow or an ocean breeze? It's not as if your cat will care about all these colours and fragrances; it's happy if the owner just empties the litter tray each day.

All producers praise their own products, sometimes referring to tests they've conducted. But it's probably best not to believe the hype and just find out what the scientists say about the different kinds of cat litter and how well they work. In the USA the researcher Debra Horwitz made an interesting study of the factors that caused some cats not to use their litter tray. She looked at more than a hundred such cats that came to her clinic over a ten-year period. They had all been to different vets to determine that there were no medical reasons behind the problems.

Their owners answered a number of questions about their cats' age, gender, toilet behaviour, medical history, type of litter used (clumping or non-clumping, perfumed or non-perfumed), whether the litter tray had a roof or not, how often the litter was changed, how many cats there were in the household, how long the problems had been going on for, and if any changes had occurred in the household (such as a house move, renovations, a new baby or additional pets).

Then the same questions were asked of 44 cat owners who visited the vet for a routine check where the cat didn't have any problems with using their litter tray. The big difference between the groups was that the cats with problems had been offered perfumed, non-clumping litter while the cats that willingly used their tray had been offered non-perfumed, clumping litter.

Cats have very sensitive noses and they don't seem to appreciate the same smells as humans do. Maybe some companies add perfume to mask the fact that the litter is of poor quality and doesn't absorb the urine very well? Regardless of the reason, the effect is the same: the cat doesn't visit the litter tray as it should. Horwitz concluded that cat litter shouldn't just be non-perfumed: it should preferably also have as little smell as possible.

Invention is big in the cat product industry. Recently, an American manufacturer created a spray which they claimed could eliminate pet odour. The idea is that you use it to spray the litter tray to neutralize the smell of ammonia and various sulphur compounds that are given off by stale urine. Nicole Cottam and Nicholas Dodman wanted to investigate whether this spray made the litter tray more attractive to cats, and whether they would urinate and defecate more inside than outside the box.

First, they studied ten cats that had never had problems using a litter tray. No difference was noticed before and after the spray was used. In the next phase of the study, they examined the behaviours and number of visits to the tray in 37 cats that sometimes failed to use the litter tray. Here they noticed a weak but positive effect of the spray: the cats went more often to the tray and were happier during their visit. A happy cat takes its time in the litter tray.

A cat shows it's unhappy when only its hindquarters are inside the tray during a visit, when it doesn't want to sit down afterwards, or when it doesn't bury its faeces with litter afterwards but gets out quickly. The conclusion of the investigation was that the spray seemed to work. But there is a much easier way of avoiding bad smells from the litter tray: use a good absorbent litter and remove clumps at least once a day.

A new form of cat litter with an extremely high absorption rate is crystal sand litter made from silica gel. It doesn't clump, but when the crystals are full they change colour. That's when you should replace all the litter. If you mix up the litter now and again (along with daily scooping of faecal material), you only need to change it once a month. Aside from the obvious benefit to cat owners, how attractive is this litter for the cats themselves, compared to clumping litter?

To find out, John Neilson visited a rehoming centre and gave 54 cats access to the two types of litter for 12 hours. They had no prior experience of any of the litter types. The cats went to the trays on 74 occasions, and only in 20 per cent of the cases did the cats prefer the crystal sand. So the clumping litter was definitely more popular.

The three studies show conclusively that clumping litter that has no smell is what most cats prefer. But it might not suit all cats. If your cat urinates or defecates outside the litter tray, it might be worth trying another type of litter for a while. If you don't have a problem, however, there is no reason for you to change. Lastly, it's possible to train some breeds to use the 'real' toilet instead of a tray. That would probably be the easiest solution ...

SCIENTISTS EXPLAIN

Which type of cat litter?

- One reason why a cat might not want to use its litter tray could be that it contains the wrong type of litter.
- Cat litter can be divided into clumping and non-clumping types. The clumping type is made out of a natural clay, bentonite, and is mined in southern Europe and the USA. The non-clumping

type is either crystal sand made out of silica or environmental pellets made out of recycled paper or sawdust.

- The best type of clumping litter is dust- and odour-free.
- Wash the whole tray with warm water and soap regularly. This is especially important if you have cats that are reluctant to use it.
- If you have non-clumping litter, you should empty the tray, wash it and fill it with new litter once a week (for pellets) or once a month (for crystal sand). Use a scoop to remove the faeces every day.
- If you have clumping litter where you daily remove urine and faeces clumps, you will need to wash the box and replace the litter only every fortnight.
- If your cat is happy about using its litter tray, keep using the same brand of litter. If you do have to change brands, do it gradually over a period to give the cat time to get used to the change.
- Study your cat's behaviour when it visits the litter tray. If it seems hesitant about using it, or if half its body is outside when it does its business, then something is wrong.
- If you have kittens, don't use too fine or clumping litter because they might sometimes eat it and become sick as a result.

The best litter tray

One of the major reasons for a cat to be left at a rehoming centre or put down is that it's not housebroken. An indoor cat needs to urinate two or three times per day and defecate once or twice a day – almost as often as an outdoor cat. The reason for cats not to visit the litter tray can be medical, but it's more likely to be because the cat litter is the wrong type or the design of the litter tray is offputting.

While much research has been done into the type of sand or litter cats prefer (see above), it's only recently that researchers have begun to study the design of the litter tray. Many cat owners prefer litter trays with a roof. They have a number of advantages: less litter ends up on the floor; the smell is less pervasive; and you don't have to look at faeces. There is a risk, however, that the owner is more likely to forget to empty a tray with a roof – out of sight, out of mind – and a tray that isn't emptied often enough can be the reason why the cat avoids going there.

In two experiments, researchers investigated whether cats preferred trays with or without roofs, or large or small trays. In the first experiment, the researchers made all the conditions exactly the same for the tray without a roof and the tray with a roof. They were emptied equally often and the best litter was used. The researchers wanted to find out what the cat, not the owner, preferred.

A total of 28 cats in 28 households were studied for 14 days. A litter tray with a roof and one without were placed next to each other, and after seven days their positions were switched. All urine clumps and faeces were gathered and weighed daily. More than half the cats had at some point in their lives used a box with a roof. Most of the cats (70 per cent) showed no preference for one type of tray over another. Four cats used the tray with the roof almost exclusively and the same number exclusively used the tray without. Bigger cats – that is, those weighing more than 6 kilograms – avoided to a larger extent the tray with the roof, perhaps because it was more difficult for them to fit inside it.

At rehoming centres and at the vet's, it's sometimes been noted that cats prefer larger trays. Do all cats prefer larger ones? Traditional litter trays in the shops vary surprisingly little in size. They are usually rectangular in shape and measure 45 to 65 centimetres long and 30 to 45 centimetres wide. These standard sizes may be for practical reasons, to not take up too much space. But what does your cat actually prefer?

The researchers conducted an experiment where cats could choose between boxes of standard size (56 cm by 34 cm and 14 cm high) and extra-large boxes (30 cm longer but otherwise of similar dimensions). In the experiment, 72 cats in 43 households were studied for 28 days. Half were female and half male,

Some big cats will avoid litter trays with a roof, while all cats prefer bigger trays without a roof to smaller boxes with a roof.

and all were neutered. A normal-sized litter tray and an extra-large one, both without a roof, were placed in the same room but as far away from each other as possible. Apart from that, the conditions were exactly the same. The trays were emptied every day and the number of urine or faeces clumps in each one was counted. After half the time had elapsed, the researchers emptied the boxes completely and switched their positions. Both before and after the researchers switched the trays, the cats preferred the larger tray. In the larger trays there were a total of 5,031 clumps, while in the normal-sized box there were only 3,239. So it's clear that, if the cat gets to decide for itself, it prefers a larger tray.

 ## SCIENTISTS EXPLAIN

The best litter tray

- The bigger the litter tray, the better the cat likes it.
- It doesn't usually matter to the cat whether the tray has a roof or not.
- Some cats have clear preferences, so if your cat isn't housebroken it's worth trying a different type of tray.
- Empty the litter tray at least once a day, and use fine-grained cat litter that clumps.
- A rule of thumb (as yet untested) is to have as many litter trays as you have cats.

Playing with your cat

Perhaps you've been to a zoo at some point and seen a leopard or a lion constantly pacing to and fro? Modern zoos are trying to avoid these stereotypical behaviours by enriching the animals' environment. For example, enclosures can be enlarged so that the cats have more opportunities to hide from attention; visitors will then be observing them more on the animals' terms. Stress levels also decrease when animals in captivity can look for food under natural conditions. That's why their meat, consisting in the wild of whole carcasses and not just a slab of meat, is hidden.

There are surprisingly few similar studies of domestic cats. What can we do to make domestic cats feel as good as possible? Can we avoid undesirable behaviours through more play and toys?

It's obvious that we try to enrich our home environment for our cats through play and petting. Cat owners in the USA spend, for example, more than 1.7 billion dollars annually on cat toys! A study of cats' play and toys was published in 2004, when Beth Strickler and Elizabeth Shull interviewed around 300 cat owners in Tennessee, USA. They asked how often and for how long the owners played with their cats, and what type of games and toys they were using.

They also wanted to investigate whether more play led to a reduction in undesirable behaviours. Cat owners using five different veterinary clinics were asked if they wanted to participate in the study. The prerequisites to participate were that the owner hadn't sought help for behaviour problems, and that the cat spent at least a part of the day outdoors.

Cat toys or activities in American households

TOY OR ACTIVITY	SHARE OF HOUSEHOLDS (PER CENT)
Cloth mouse	62
Cloth mouse with catnip	62
Ball with a bell	64
Cuddly toy	59
Scratching post	55
Cardboard box	50
Ball without a bell	49
String	41
Paper bag	40
Rod with feathers	39
Feather	33
Scouting for birds	26
Massage	22
Hide and seek	18
Laser pointer	14
Cat bag that rustles	12
Grass	9
Hair band	9
Scratching a tree	9

About the same number of males as females were in the study, most of them were neutered, and their average age was five years. Two out of three cats in the study never went outside. Around a third of the cats were declawed, that is, a vet had surgically removed the cat's claws – the operation is allowed in certain American states, but not in the UK. An average household in Tennessee offered the cat eight different toys or activities (see table above).

Most owners played with their cat more than twice a day, with each play session usually lasting five to ten minutes. Female cats displayed fewer unwanted behaviours than male cats, regardless of whether they were neutered or not. The most common problem was that the males urinated indoors in other locations than the litter tray. When the researchers compared the number of unwanted behaviours – aggression towards visitors, aggression towards the owner, fights with other cats outdoors, fights with friendly cats indoors, defecating and/or urinating outside the litter tray – it transpired that the number of toys and activities the cats had access to didn't matter.

Frequency of play with the owner had no influence either. However, longer periods of play were crucial to prevent unwanted behaviours. Each play session needed to be at least five minutes long but preferably 15–30 minutes for the cat to feel better and decrease the number of its unwanted behaviours.

Of all the activities and toys offered to the cats, it was the string that turned out to be the most effective. Chasing a length of string pulled along the floor or jumping up to catch a dangling string were the play activities that seemed to satisfy most cats, to the extent that the number of undesirable behaviours decreased.

If you've ever wondered why your cat no longer plays with the cloth mouse or the ball that was so popular last week, it's because cats get used to (read: get bored with) playing with the same toy after a few days. Several studies have shown that the same cat toys shouldn't be available all the time; a more successful strategy is to bring out different toys on a rotating schedule.

 **SCIENTISTS EXPLAIN**

Playing with your cat

- You can reduce the number of unwanted behaviours by playing with your cat and giving it plenty of attention.
- Female cats display far fewer unwanted behaviours indoors than males.
- The most common undesirable behaviours are urinating indoors in places other than the litter tray and aggression towards the owner.
- Play with your cat for at least five minutes, and preferably 15–30 minutes, every day.
- A length of string is the most fun and effective toy for a cat.
- Don't keep toys out when the cat no longer shows any interest in them. It's better to put them away and then take them out again later.

References

General

European Pet Food Industry Federation, 2012. Facts & Figures 2012.
Statistiska Centralbyrån (Central Bureau of Statistics), 2012.
'Hundar, katter och andra sällskapsdjur' ('Dogs, cats and other pets') 2012.

Introduction

Aspenström, W. 1965. 'Gula tassen. En liten historia berättad och ritad för Pontus det minnesvärda året 1961' [Yellow bag. A little story told and designed for Pontus, in the memorable year 1961]. Rabén & Sjögren.
Berg, A. 2015. 'En tass i litteraturens tjänst' [A paw in the service of literature]. – *Dagens Nyheter*, 21 March 2015. Download here: http://www.dn.se/kultur-noje/en-tass-i-litteraturens-tjanst/
Eliot, T. S. 1939. *Old Possum's Book of Practical Cats*. Faber & Faber 2010.

Gosling, L. et al. 2013. 'What is a feral cat? Variation in definitions may be associated with different management strategies.' – *Journal of Feline Medicine and Surgery* 15: 759–764.

Lessing, D. 2002. *On Cats.* Harper Perennial 2008.

Söderström, B. 2009. 'Snöleopard – Sällsamtmöte Tsagaan i Tost.' – *Fauna & Flora* 104: 2–11.

Söderström, B. 2012. 'Naturmorgon i p1 den 25 februari.' Download here: http://sverigesradio.se/sida/avsnitt/

1 The wild in the tame

More wild than tame?

Driscoll, C. A. et al. 2009. 'From wild animals to domestic pets, an evolutionary view of domestication.' – *Proceedings of the National Academy of Sciences of the United States of America* 106: 9971–9978.

Gosling, L. et al. 2013. 'What is a feral cat? Variation in definitions may be associated with different management strategies.' – *Journal of Feline Medicine and Surgery* 15: 759–764.

Grimm, D. 2014. 'The genes that turned wildcats into kitty cats.' – *Science* 346: 6211.

Kurushima, J. D. et al. 2013. 'Variation of cats under domestication: Genetic assignment of domestic cats to breeds and worldwide random-bred populations.' – *Animal Genetics* 44: 311–324.

Lipinski, M. J. et al. 2008. 'The ascent of cat breeds: Genetic evaluations of breeds and worldwide random-bred populations.' – *Genomics* 91: 12–21.

Montague, M. J. et al. 2014. 'Comparative analysis of the domestic cat genome reveals genetic signatures underlying feline biology and domestication.' – *Proceedings of the National Academy of Sciences of the United States of America* 111: 17230–17235.

Pontier, D. & Natoli E. 1999. 'Infanticide in rural male cats (*Felis catus* L.) as a reproductive mating tactic.' – *Aggressive Behavior* 25: 445–499.

How many cats should I have?
Bernstein, P. L. & Strack, M. 1996. 'A game of cat and house: Spatial patterns and behavior of 14 domestic cats (*Felis catus*) in the home.' – *Anthrozoös* 9: 25–39.

Pachel, C. L. 2014. 'Intercat aggression: Restoring harmony in the home.' – *Veterinary Clinics of North America: Small Animal Practice* 44: 565–579.

Pontier, D. et al. 2000. 'The impact of behavioral plasticity at individual level on domestic cat population dynamics.' – *Ecological Modelling* 133: 117–124.

Ramos, D. et al. 2013. 'Are cats (*Felis catus*) from multi-cat households more stressed? Evidence from assessment of fecal glucocorticoid metabolite analysis.' – *Physiology and Behavior* 122: 72–75.

van den Bos, R. 1998. 'Post-conflict stress response in confined group-living cats (*Felis silvestris catus*)'. – *Applied Animal Behaviour Science* 59: 323–330.

Who is Top Cat?
Barry, K. J. & Crowell-Davis, S. L. 1999. 'Gender differences in the social behavior of the neutered indoor-only domestic cat.' – *Applied Animal Behaviour Science* 64: 193–211.

Bonanni, R. et al. 2007. 'Feeding-order in an urban feral domestic cat colony: Relationship to dominance rank, sex and age.' – *Animal Behaviour* 74: 1369–1379.

Moesta, A. & Crowell-Davis, S. 2011. 'Intercat aggression: General considerations, prevention and treatment.' – *Tierärztliche Praxis Kleintiere* 39: 97–104.

Natoli, E. et al. 2001. 'Male and female agonistic and affiliative relationships in a social group of farm cats (*Felis catus* L.).' – *Behavioural Processes* 53: 137–143.

Natoli, E. et al. 2007. 'Male reproductive success in a social group of urban feral cats (*Felis catus* L.).' – *Ethology* 113: 283–289.

van den Bos, R. & de Cock Buning, T. 1994. 'Social behaviour of domestic cats (*Felis lybica f. catus* L.): A study of dominance in a group of female laboratory cats.' – *Ethology* 98: 14–37.

The cats' home area

Barratt, D. G. 1997. 'Home range size, habitat utilisation and movement patterns of suburban and farm cats *Felis catus*.' – *Ecography* 20: 271–280.

Ferreira, J. P. et al. 2011. 'Human-related factors regulate the spatial ecology of domestic cats in sensitive areas for conservation.' – *PLoS ONE* 6: e25970.

Hervias, S. et al. 2014. 'Assessing the impact of introduced cats on island biodiversity by combining dietary and movement analysis.' – *Journal of Zoology* 292: 39–47.

Horn, J. A. et al. 2011. 'Home range, habitat use, and activity patterns of free-roaming domestic cats.' – *Journal of Wildlife Management* 75: 1177–1185.

Kitts-Morgan, S. E. et al. 2015. 'Free-ranging farm cats: Home range size and predation on a livestock unit in northwest Georgia.' – *PLoS ONE* 10: e0120513.

Liberg, O. 1980. 'Spacing patterns in a population of rural free roaming domestic cats.' – *Oikos* 35: 336–349.

Metsers, E. M. et al. 2010. 'Cat-exclusion zones in rural and urban-fringe landscapes: How large would they have to be?' – *Wildlife Research* 37: 47–56.

Recio, M. R. et al. 2014. 'Quantifying finescale resource selection by introduced feral cats to complement management decision-making in ecologically sensitive areas.' – *Biological Invasions* 16: 1915–1927.

Thomas, R. L. et al. 2014. 'Ranging characteristics of the domestic cat (*Felis catus*) in an urban environment.' – *Urban Ecosystems* 17: 911–921.

The predatory cat

Biben, M. 1979. 'Predation and predatory play behaviour of domestic cats.' – *Animal Behaviour* 27: 81–94.

Bonnington, C. et al. 2013. 'Fearing the feline: Domestic cats reduce avian fecundity through trait-mediated indirect effects that increase nest predation by other species.' – *Journal of Applied Ecology* 50: 15–24.

Calver, M. et al. 2007. 'Reducing the rate of predation on wildlife by pet cats: The efficacy and practicability of collar-mounted pounce protectors.' – *Biological Conservation* 137: 341–348.

Hervias, S. et al. 2014. 'Assessing the impact of introduced cats on island biodiversity by combining dietary and movement analysis.' – *Journal of Zoology* 292: 39–47.

Hughes, B. J. et al. 2008. 'Cats and seabirds: Effects of feral domestic cat *Felis silvestris catus* eradication on the population of sooty terns *Onychoprion fuscata* on Ascension Island, South Atlantic.' – *Ibis* 150 (Suppl. 1): 122–131.

Kitts-Morgan, S. E. et al. 2015. 'Free-ranging farm cats: Home range size and predation on a livestock unit in northwest Georgia.' – *PLoS ONE* 10: e0120513.

Krauze-Gryz, D. et al. 2012. 'Predation by domestic cats in rural areas of central Poland: An assessment based on two methods.' – *Journal of Zoology* 288: 260–266.

Liberg, O. 1984. 'Food habits and prey impact by feral and house-based domestic cats in a rural area in southern Sweden.' – *Journal of Mammology* 65: 424–432.

Loss, S. R. et al. 2013. 'The impact of free-ranging domestic cats on wildlife of the United States.' – *Nature Communications* 4: 1396.

Loyd, K. A. T. et al. 2013. 'Quantifying free-roaming domestic cat predation using animal-borne video cameras.' – *Biological Conservation* 160: 183–189.

Recio, M. R. et al. 2014. 'Quantifying finescale resource selection by introduced feral cats to complement management decision-making in ecologically sensitive areas.' – *Biological Invasions* 16: 1915–1927.

Robertson, I. 1998. 'Survey of predation by domestic cats.' – *Australian Veterinary Journal* 76: 551–554.

Silva-Rodriguez, E. A. & Sieving, K. E. 2011. 'Influence of care of domestic carnivores on their predation on vertebrates.' – *Conservation Biology* 25: 808–815.

Svensson. S. 1996. 'Huskattens predation p. fåglar i Sverige' [Housecats' predation on birds in Sweden]. – *Ornis Svecica* 6: 127–130.

Thomas, R. L. et al. 2012. 'Spatio-temporal variation in predation by urban domestic cats (*Felis catus*) and the acceptability of possible management actions in the UK.' – *PLoS ONE* 7: e49369.

Thomas, R. L. et al. 2014. 'Ranging characteristics of the domestic cat (*Felis catus*) in an urban environment.' – *Urban Ecosystems* 17: 911–921.

The mating season

Natoli, E. et al. 2000. 'Mate choice in the domestic cat (*Felis silvestris catus* L.).' – *Aggressive Behavior* 26: 455–465.

Pontier, D. & Natoli E. 1999. 'Infanticide in rural male cats (*Felis catus* L.) as a reproductive mating tactic.' – *Aggressive Behavior* 25: 445–449.

Say, L. et al. 1999. 'High variation in multiple paternity of domestic cats (*Felis catus* L.) in relation to environmental conditions.' – *Proceedings of the Royal Society of London*, Series B 266: 2071–2074.

Say, L. et al. 2001. 'Influence of oestrus synchronization on male reproductive success in the domestic cat (*Felis catus* L.).' – *Proceedings of the Royal Society of London*, Series B 268: 1049–1053.

2 Your cat's senses

The cat's memory

Fiset, S. & Doré, F. Y. 2006. 'Duration of cats' (*Felis catus*) working memory for disappearing objects.' – *Animal Cognition* 9: 62–70.

Kraus, C. et al. 2014. 'Distractible dogs, constant cats? A test of the distraction hypothesis in two domestic species.' – *Animal Behaviour* 93: 173–181.

Does your cat listen to you?

McComb, K. et al. 2014. 'Elephants can determine ethnicity, gender, and age from acoustic cues in human voices.' – *Proceedings of the National Academy of Sciences of the United States of America* 111: 5433–5438.

Merola, I. et al. 2015. 'Social referencing and cat–human communication.' – *Animal Cognition* 18: 639–648.

Mills, D. S. et al. 2000. 'Evaluation of the welfare implications and efficacy of an ultrasonic "deterrent" for cats.' – *Veterinary Record* 147: 678–680.

Potter, A. & Mills, D. S. 2015. 'Domestic cats (*Felis silvestris catus*) do not show signs of secure attachment to their owners.' – *PLoS ONE* 10: e0135109.

Saito, A. & Shinozuka, K. 2013. 'Vocal recognition of owners by domestic cats (*Felis catus*).' – *Animal Cognition* 16: 685–690.

The sounds cats make

Frazer Sissom, D. E. et al. 1991. 'How cats purr.' – *Journal of Zoology* 223: 67–78.

McComb, K. et al. 2009. 'The cry embedded within the purr.' – *Current Biology* 19: 507–508.

Nicastro, N. & Owren, M. J. 2003. 'Classification of domestic cat (*Felis catus*) vocalizations by naive and experienced human listeners.' – *Journal of Comparative Psychology* 117: 44–52.

Yeon, S. C. et al. 2011. 'Differences between vocalization evoked by social stimuli in feral cats and house cats.' – *Behavioural Processes* 87: 183–189.

The cat's sense of smell

Nakabayashi, M. et al. 2012. 'Do faecal odours enable domestic cats (*Felis catus*) to distinguish familiarity of the donors?' – *Journal of Ethology* 30: 325–329.

Salazar, I. et al. 1996. 'The vomeronasal organ of the cat.' – *Journal of Anatomy* 188: 445–454.

Staples L. G. et al. 2008. 'Rats discriminate individual cats by their odor: Possible involvement of the accessory olfactory system.' – *Neuroscience & Biobehavioral Reviews* 32: 1209–1217.

The cat's walking style

Bishop, K. L. et al. 2008. 'Whole body mechanics of stealthy walking in cats.' – *PLoS ONE* 3: e3808.

G.lvez-L.pez, E. et al. 2011. 'The search for stability on narrow supports: An experimental study in cats and dogs.' – *Zoology* 114: 224–232.

3 Your cat's behaviour

Urine markings

Borchelt, P. L. & Voith, V. L. 1982. 'Diagnosis and treatment of elimination behavior problems in cats.' – *Veterinary Clinics of North America: Small Animal Practice* 12: 673–681.

Feldman, H. N. 1994. 'Methods of scent marking in the domestic cat.' – *Canadian Journal of Zoology* 72: 1093–1099.

Mellen, J. D. 1993. 'A comparative analysis of scent-marking, social and reproductive behavior in 20 species of small cats (*Felis*).' – *American Zoologist* 33: 151–166.

Ruiz-Olmo, J. et al. 2013. 'Substrate selection for urine spraying in captive wildcats.' – *Journal of Zoology* 290: 143–150.

Scratching

Feldman, H. N. 1994. 'Methods of scent marking in the domestic cat.' – *Canadian Journal of Zoology* 72: 1093–1099.

Mengoli, M. et al. 2013. 'Scratching behavior and its features: A questionnaire-based study in an Italian sample of domestic cats.' – *Journal of Feline Medicine and Surgery* 15: 886–892.

Tail in the air

Cafazzo, S. & Natoli, E. 2009. 'The social function of tail up in the domestic cat (*Felis silvestris catus*).' – *Behavioural Processes* 80: 60–66.

Where your cat wants to be stroked

Ellis, S. L. H. et al. 2014. 'The influence of body region, handler familiarity and order of region handled on the domestic cat's response to being stroked.' – *Applied Animal Behaviour Science.* http://dx.doi.org/10.1016/j.applanim.2014.11.002

Gourkow, N. & Fraser, D. 2006. 'The effect of housing and handling practices on the welfare, behaviour and selection of domestic cats (*Felis sylvestris catus*) by adopters in animal shelter.' – *Animal Welfare* 15: 371–377.

Soennichsen, S. & Chamove, A. S. 2002. 'Responses of cats to petting by humans.' – *Anthrozoös* 15: 258–265.

Hairballs

Cannon, M. 2013. 'Hairballs in cats: A normal nuisance or a sign that something is wrong?' – *Journal of Feline Medicine and Surgery* 15: 21–29.

Grooming

Curtis, T. M. et al. 2003. 'Influence of familiarity and relatedness on proximity and allogrooming in domestic cats (*Felis catus*).' – *American Journal of Veterinary Research* 64: 1151–1154.

Eckstein, R. A. & Hart, B. L. 2000. 'The organization and control of grooming in cats.' – *Applied Animal Behaviour Science* 68: 131–140.

Randall, W. 1988. 'Grooming reflexes in the cat: Endocrine and pharmacological studies.' – *Annals of New York Academy of Sciences* 525: 301–320.

van den Bos, R. 1998. The function of allogrooming in domestic cats (*Felis silvestris catus*): A study in a group of cats living in confinement.' – *Journal of Ethology* 16: 1–13.

van den Bos, R. 1998. 'Post-conflict stress-response in confined group-living cats (*Felis silvestris catus*).' – *Applied Animal Behaviour Science* 59: 323–330.

4 Your cat's temperament

A secure upbringing

Lowe, S. E. & Bradshaw, J. W. S. 2002. 'Responses of pet cats to being held by an unfamiliar person, from weaning to three years of age.' – *Anthrozoös* 15: 69–79.

McCune, S. 1995. 'The impact of paternity and early socialisation on the development of cats' behaviour to people and novel objects.' – *Applied Animal Behaviour Science* 45: 109–124.

Cats' charisma

Gartner, M. C. & Weiss, A. 2013. 'Personality in felids: A review.' – *Applied Animal Behaviour Science* 144: 1–13.

Gartner, M. C. et al. 2014. 'Personality structure in the domestic cat (*Felis silvestris catus*), Scottish wildcat (*Felis silvestris grampia*), clouded leopard (*Neofelis nebulosa*), snow leopard (*Panthera uncia*), and African lion (*Panthera leo*): A comparative study.' – *Journal of Comparative Psychology* 128: 414–426.

Gosling, S. D. & Bonnenburg, A. V. 1998. 'An integrative approach to personality research in anthrozoology: Ratings of six species of pets and their owners.' – *Anthrozoös* 11: 148–156.

Lee, C. M. et al. 2007. 'Personality in domestic cats.' – *Psychological Reports* 100: 27–29.

Aggressive cats

Amat, M. et al. 2009. 'Potential risk factors associated with feline behaviour problems.' – *Applied Animal Behaviour Science* 121: 134–139.

Bain, M. & Stelow, E. 2014. 'Feline aggression toward family members: A guide for practitioners.' – *Veterinary Clinics of North America: Small Animal Practice* 44: 581–597.

Crowell-Davis, S. L. et al. 1997. 'Social behaviour and aggressive problems of cats.' – *Veterinary Clinics of North America: Small Animal Practice* 27: 549–568.

Luescher, U. A. et al. 1991. 'Stereotypic or obsessive-compulsive disorders in dogs and cats.' – *Veterinary Clinics of North America: Small Animal Practice* 21: 401–413.

Palacio, J. et al. 2007. 'Incidence of and risk factors for cat bites: A first step in prevention and treatment of feline aggression.' – *Journal of Feline Medicine and Surgery* 9: 188–195.

Reisner, I. R. et al. 1994. 'Friendliness to humans and defensive aggression in cats: The influence of handling and paternity.' – *Psychology & Behavior* 55: 1119–1124.

At the rehoming centre

Broadley, H. M. et al. 2014. 'Effect of single-cat versus multi-cat home history on perceived behavioral stress in domestic cats (*Felis silvestris catus*) in an animal shelter.' – *Journal of Feline Medicine and Surgery* 16: 137–143.

Delgado, M. M. et al. 2012. 'Human perceptions of coat color as an indicator of domestic cat personality.' – *Anthrozoos* 25: 427–440.

Eriksson, P. et al. 2009. 'A survey of cat shelters in Sweden.' – *Animal Welfare* 18: 283–288.

Gouveia, K. et al. 2011. 'The behaviour of domestic cats in a shelter: Residence time, density and sex ratio.' – *Applied Animal Behaviour Science* 130: 53–59.

Hirsch, E. N. et al. 2014. 'Swedish cat shelters: A descriptive survey of husbandry practices, routines and management.' – *Animal Welfare* 23: 411–421.

Loberg, J. & Lundmark, F. 2013. 'Grupph.llning av katt: Hur p.verkar golvyta per katt katternas beteende i stabila, store grupper?' [Group behavior in cats: How does floor space affect the behaviour of cats in stable large groups?] – Final Report to the Swedish Board of Agriculture. Ref. 31–4662/10.

Scheller, A. 2013. 'Black cats less than half as likely to be adopted as gray cats.' – *Huffington Post*, 21 October 2013.

Stelow, E. A. et al. 2015. 'The relationship between coat color and aggressive behaviors in the domestic cat.' – *Journal of Applied Animal Welfare Science*. doi: 10.1080/10888705. 2015.10081820

Vinke, C. M. et al. 2014. 'Will a hiding box provide stress reduction for shelter cats?' – *Applied Animal Behaviour Science* 160: 86–93.

At the vet's

Berdoy, M. et al. 2000. 'Fatal attraction in rats infected with *Toxoplasma gondii*.' – *Proceedings of the Royal Society, London, Series B* 267: 1591–1594.

Brondani, J. T. et al. 2011. 'Refinement and initial validation of a multidimensional composite scale for use in assessing acute postoperative pain in cats.' – *American Journal of Veterinary Research* 72: 174–183.

Kuiken, T. et al. 2004. 'Avian H5N1 influenza in cats.' – *Science* 306: 241.

Natoli, E. et al. 2005. 'Bold attitude makes male urban feral domestic cats more vulnerable to Feline Immunodeficiency Virus.' – *Neuroscience & Biobehavioral Sciences* 29: 151–157.

Rochlitz, I. 2003. 'Study of factors that may predispose domestic cats to road traffic accidents: Part 1.' – *Veterinary Record* 153: 549–553.

Rochlitz, I. 2004. 'The effects of road traffic accidents on domestic cats and their owners.' – *Animal Welfare* 13: 51–55.

Zeiler, G. E. et al. 2014. 'Assessment of behavioural changes in domestic cats during short-term hospitalisation.' – *Journal of Feline Medicine and Surgery* 16: 499–503.

5 The cat and the human

Like cats and dogs

Feuerstein, N. & Terkel, J. 2008. 'Interrelationships of dogs (*Canis familiaris*) and cats (*Felis catus* L.) living under the same roof.' – *Applied Animal Behaviour Science* 113: 150–165.

Silvestro, D. et al. 2015. 'The role of clade competition in the diversification of North American canids.' – *Proceedings of the National Academy of Sciences of the United States of America* 112: 8684– 8689.

The cat's effect on our health

Burnham, D. et al. 2002. 'What's new pussycat? On talking to babies and animals.' – *Science* 296: 1435.

Edney, A. T. B. 1992. 'Companion animals and human health.' – *Veterinary Records* 130: 285–287.

Edney, A. T. 1994. 'Companion animals and human health: An overview.' – *Journal of the Royal Society of Medicine* 88: 704–708.

Friedmann, E. & Thomas, S. A. 1995. 'Pet ownership, social support, and one-year survival after acute myocardial infarction in the Cardiac Arrhythmia Suppression Trial (CAST).' – *American Journal of Cardiology* 76: 1213–1217.

Leigh, D. 1966. 'The psychology of the pet owner.' – *Journal of Small Animal Practice* 7: 517–522.

Mathers, M. et al. 2010. 'Pet ownership and adolescent health: Cross-sectional population study.' – *Journal of Paediatrics and Child Health* 46: 729–735.

Mertens, C. 1995. 'The human–cat relationship.' – *Tierärztliche Umschau* 50: 71–75.

Myrick, J. G. 2015. 'Emotion regulation, procrastination, and watching cat videos online: Who watches Internet cats, why, and to what effect?' – *Computers in Human Behavior* 52: 168–176.

Nittono, H. et al. 2012. 'The power of Kawaii: Viewing cute images promotes a careful behavior and narrows attentional focus.' – *PLoS ONE* 7: e46362.

Serpell, J. 1991. 'Beneficial effects of pet ownership on some aspects of human health and behaviour.' – *Journal of the Royal Society of Medicine* 84: 717–720.

Stammbach, K. B. & Turner, D. C. 1999. 'Understanding the human–cat relationship: Human social support or attachment.' – *Anthrozoös* 12: 162–168.

Zasloff, R. L. & Kidd, A. H. 1994. 'Attachment to feline companions.' – *Psychological Reports* 74: 747–752.

The cat's health and wellbeing

Bradshaw, J. W. S. & Casey, R.A. 2007. 'Anthropomorphism and anthropocentrism as influences in the quality of life of companion animals.' – *Animal Welfare* 16: 149–154.

Chartrand, T. L. et al. 2008. 'Automatic effects of anthropomorphized objects on behavior.' – *Social Cognition* 26: 198–209.

Crowell-Davis, S. L. 2008. 'Motivation for pet ownership and its relevance to behavior problems.' – *Compendium* 30: 423–428.

Gelberg, H. B. 2013. 'Diagnostic exercise: Sudden behavior change in a cat.' – *Veterinary Pathology* 50: 1156–1157.

Heidenberger, E. 1997. 'Housing conditions and behavioural problems of indoor cats as assessed by their owners.' – *Applied Animal Behaviour Science* 52: 345–364.

Jongman, E. C. 2007. 'Adaptation of domestic cats to confinement.' – *Journal of Veterinary Behavior* 2: 193–196.

Kienzle, E. & Bergler, R. 2006. 'Human–animal relationship of owners of normal and overweight cats.' – *Journal of Nutrition* 136: 1947–1950.

Lowe, S. E. & Bradshaw, J. W. S. 2001. 'Ontogeny of individuality in the domestic cat in the home environment.' – *Animal Behaviour* 61: 231–237.

Piccione, G. et al. 2013. 'Daily rhythm of total activity pattern in domestic cats (*Felis silvestris catus*) maintained in two different housing conditions.' – *Journal of Veterinary Behavior* 8: 189–194.

Rochlitz, I. 2005. 'A review of the housing requirements of domestic cats (*Felis silvestris catus*) kept in the home.' – *Applied Animal Behaviour Science* 93: 97–109.

Schultz, S. 2000. 'Pets and their humans. Domesticated animals have evolved to make their desires known.' – *US News & World Report* 129: 53–55.

Sonntag, Q. & Overall, K . L. 2014. 'Key determinants of dog and cat welfare: Behaviour, breeding and household lifestyle.' – *Revue Scientifique et Technique* 33: 213–220.

Turner, D. C. et al. 1986. 'Variation in domestic cat behaviour towards humans: A paternal effect.' – *Animal Behaviour* 34: 1890–1892.

Wedl, M. et al. 2011. 'Factors influencing the temporal patterns of dyadic behaviours and interactions between domestic cats and their owners.' – *Behavioural Processes* 86: 58–67.

Wemelsfelder, F. 2007. 'How animals communicate quality of life: The qualitative assessment of behaviour.' – *Animal Welfare* 16: 25–31.

Wiseman, R. et al. 1998. 'Can animals detect when their owners are returning home? An experimental test of the "psychic pet" phenomenon.' – *British Journal of Psychology* 89: 453–462.

6 The cat at home

Food preferences

Bradshaw, J. W. S. & Cook, S. E. 1996. 'Patterns of pet cat behaviour at feeding occasions.' – *Applied Animal Behaviour Science* 47: 61–74.

Bradshaw, J. W. S. et al. 1996. 'Food selection by the domestic cat, an obligate carnivore.' – *Comparative Biochemistry and Physiology* 114A: 205–209.

Bradshaw, J. W. S. et al. 2000. 'Differences in food preferences between individuals and populations of domestic cats *Felis silvestris catus*.' – *Applied Animal Behaviour Science* 68: 257–268.

Church S. C. et al. 1996. 'Frequency-dependent food selection by domestic cats: A comparative study.' – *Ethology* 102: 495–509.

MacDonald, M. L. et al. 1984. 'Nutrition of the domestic cat, a mammalian carnivore.' – *Annual Review of Nutrition* 4: 521–562.

Mongillo, P. et al. 2012. 'Successful treatment of abnormal feeding behavior in a cat.' – *Journal of Veterinary Behavior* 7: 390–393.

Wei, A. et al. 2011. 'Effect of water content in a canned food on voluntary food intake and body weight in cats.' – *American Journal of Veterinary Research* 72: 918–923.

How cats lap

Reis, P. M. et al. 2010. 'How cats lap: Water uptake by *Felis catus*.' – Science 330: 1231–1234.

Which type of cat litter?

Borchelt, P. L. 1991. 'Cat elimination behavior problems.' – *Veterinary Clinics of North America: Small Animal Practice* 21: 257–264.

Cottam, N. & Dodman, N. H. 2007. 'Effect of an odor eliminator on feline litter box behavior.' – *Journal of Feline Medicine and Surgery* 9: 44–50.

Horwitz, D. F. 1997. 'Behavioral and environmental factors associated with elimination behavior problems in cats: A retrospective study.' – *Applied Animal Behaviour Science* 52: 129–137.

Neilson, J. 2004. 'Thinking outside the box: Feline elimination.' – *Journal of Feline Medicine and Surgery* 6: 5–11.

The best litter tray

Grigg, E. K. et al. 2013. 'Litter box preference in domestic cat: Covered versus uncovered.' – *Journal of Feline Medicine and Surgery* 15: 280–284.

Guy, N. C. et al. 2014. 'Litterbox size preference in domestic cats (*Felis catus*).' – *Journal of Veterinary Behavior* 9: 78–82.

Playing with your cat

Strickler, B. L. & Shull, E. A. 2014. 'An owner survey of toys, activities, and behavior problems in indoor cats.' – *Journal of Veterinary Behavior* 9: 207–214.

West, M. J. 1977. 'Exploration and play with objects in domestic kittens.' – *Developmental Psychobiology* 10: 53–57.

Index

Acknowledgements

FIRST AND FOREMOST, I'd like to thank my children, Love and Alicia, and my wife Katarina Andreasen, for their positive encouragement and support when I was inside the writing bubble. Katarina gave me many great suggestions for improving the text. Many thanks! Our three cats, Sepia, Chai and Simba, have kept me company by – and on – the computer. They also let me know when it was time for me to take a break from writing.

Anders Rådén made the stylish and accurate illustrations in the book. Lastly, a big thank you to my publisher Martin Ransgart and my editor Maria Ulaner. It has been a privilege to work with you all.